The
INTRANET
MANAGEMENT
H A N D B O O K

The
INTRANET
MANAGEMENT
HANDBOOK

Martin White

Information Today, Inc.

Medford, New Jersey

First printing, 2011

The Intranet Management Handbook

Copyright © 2011 by Martin White

First U.K. publication by Facet Publishing, 2011
Simultaneous U.S. publication by Information Today, Inc., 2011

Library of Congress Cataloging-in-Publication Data

White, Martin S. (Martin Scott), 1948-
The intranet management handbook / Martin White.
    p. cm.
Summary: "Offers a wealth of practical advice on intranet management, based on the work of the author as an intranet consultant over the past fifteen years"-- Provided by publisher.
Includes bibliographical references and index.
ISBN 978-1-57387-426-7
1. Intranets (Computer networks)--Management. I. Title.
HD30.385.W45 2011
004.6'82068--dc22

2011006050

Printed and bound in the United States of America

Cover design by Danielle Nicotra

www.infotoday.com

For W. Gordon Graham

Contents

Foreword

As Martin highlights, there are perhaps a million intranets in the world, but very few books to guide the work of those responsible for managing all these sites. What the intranet community (and industry) needs are good intranet books; thankfully this is such a book.

Intranets are not like websites. Hidden away within organizations, it is difficult for teams to learn from others, and to avoid reinventing the wheel. This has been the biggest contributor to the relatively slow pace of intranet evolution, leaving internal (enterprise) sites lagging far behind publicly visible websites.

Organizations cannot survive without their intranets. Without these invaluable internal sites, there would be no place to house the thousands of forms, policies, instructions, tips, guidelines, processes and tools that make organizations tick.

While no organization I know would seriously consider turning off their intranets, few sites are truly loved. They are often taken for granted, sometimes ignored, and very rarely given the resources to flourish.

Part of the problem is that even the teams that run intranets struggle to succinctly articulate the value and importance of their sites. It can also be hard to uncover best practices that support much-needed business cases and resource requests.

For all these reasons, I would argue that the starting point for delivering successful and valuable intranets is to better share expertise within the intranet community. One of the most effective ways of doing this is via books such as this one.

I've known Martin for quite a few years now, and he started working on intranets long before that. There are few who can claim more than a decade's professional intranet experience, making Martin ideally placed to write this book.

On behalf of the intranet community, I thank Martin for writing such a useful book, and look forward to the positive impact it will have on teams around the globe.

James Robertson
Step Two Designs
Sydney, Australia

Preface

How many intranets are there that need the skills and vision of an intranet manager? It is a very difficult question to answer. In the UK, information from the e-business survey conducted annually by the Office for National Statistics indicates that at the end of 2008 there were certainly over 50,000 intranets in businesses with more than ten employees. There will certainly be more in other types of organization. Every intranet needs a manager, even if managing the intranet is only one of their roles. Scale the UK figures up to the European Union and add in North America, and the installed base might easily be of the order of a million or more intranets. That is a lot of potential readers for books on how to ensure that the organization is getting the best from its intranet. Yet look along the shelves of any major bookshop and only rarely will there be even one book on intranet management. A search on the term 'intranet' on Amazon.co.uk will, in the first 24 titles, include 12 published before 2000.

Now that this book has been published, both I and Facet Publishing will be interested to find out whether this is an untapped market, or whether all the problems have been solved and no one needs any advice. We both hope that it is the former!

I should say at the outset that I have never managed an intranet, but over the last ten years I have worked on nearly a hundred intranet projects and talked to a very large number of intranet managers at conferences and workshops around the world. I have learned much from these projects and encounters, including that there is still no such thing as best practice in intranet management. Almost always the objective of the projects I have undertaken, be they in the USA or Kuwait, has been the development of an intranet strategy.

This book sets out how I go about developing an intranet strategy. One of my heroes is the Nobel physicist Richard Feynman, and his view of his work is that he was creating a tool-box of mathematical tricks that others could use in the development of something useful. This book contains some of my consulting tricks, which I hope that readers will be able to adapt to their own particular requirements.

The approach I have taken is one that aligns to my profession as an information scientist. For 40 years I have been fascinated by how people find, evaluate and use information. There has of course been a great deal of academic research into these topics, but very little specific to intranets. This is probably because of the inevitable issues about confidentiality, something that until fairly recently has been a barrier to the development of intranet communities. This approach manifests itself in regarding an intranet as a decision-support application. Good decisions need to be based on good information, to which experience and expertise can then be added.

There is very little technology in this book, even in the chapter on technology. The focus is on intranet management, and how to make the decisions that will determine the value and impact of an intranet in an organization. To try to define the scope of this book I have tried to set out in each chapter a competency that I feel an intranet manager should possess. The only major omission is the management of intranet design, as this is the subject of a book by James Robertson which has recently been published by Step Two Designs.

Even after ten years I remain fascinated by intranets and the way that they reflect organizational culture, structure, objectives and the ambitions of the people who work in the organization. Above all, they reflect the way in which the organization regards information as an asset and seeks to use this asset in the service of stakeholders. That should be the role of the chief information officer, but, sadly, that is often not the case. The responsibility for maximizing the use of the information in the intranet then falls to the intranet manager, and here, almost without exception, I have found people with a passion for the tasks they perform and the challenges they face.

Hopefully, one day the career progression of an intranet manager will lead to a position on the main board, rather than sideways to another organization. That will be a true indicator of intranet – and information – management maturity.

Martin White

Acknowledgements

I owe a very considerable debt to colleagues and clients who have contributed to this book by shaping and challenging my views of intranet management over the last decade. In particular I would like to thank Bob Boiko, Janus Boye, Jed Cawthorne, Caroline Coetzee, Christine Cornelius, Maria Dadras, Helen Day, Richard Dennison, David Gilroy, Peter Kibby, Simone Kluener, Jane McConnell, Howard McQueen, Mark Morell, James Robertson and his colleagues at Step Two Designs, Ian Roddis, Michael Sampson, Toby Ward, Nicky Waters and Christiane Wolff.

Jane, James, Michael and Richard have kindly allowed me to quote from their work.

Invitations to participate in conferences and communities hosted by Janus Boye (JBoye) and Kurt Kragh Sørensen (IntraTeam) have been invaluable. Paul Miller (Intranet Benchmarking Forum) commissioned two reports into the use of SharePoint for intranets, the research for which added substantially to my understanding of the management challenges of SharePoint. At Information Today in the USA Michelle Manafy has been very supportive of my Behind the Firewall intranet column in *EContent* magazine and for many years Jane Dysart has been instrumental in enabling me to participate in the KMWorld/Intranets conferences in San Jose CA, Washington DC and New York. My colleagues in the Information School at the University of Sheffield have given me the opportunity to lecture to students on intranets, content management and information management.

Helen Carley at Facet Publishing has tried for more than five years to persuade me to write a book on intranets. I hope that I have met her expectations.

This book is dedicated to W. Gordon Graham, a distinguished former Chairman of Butterworth Publishing, who over the last 30 years has encouraged me in my writing and imbued me with his love of books and book publishing.

Most important of all, my wife Cynthia and my sons Nick and Simon have been immensely supportive during the writing of this and my five previous books. This is a public announcement that there will not be a seventh!

Part 1
Foundations

1

Managing intranets: opportunities and challenges

Life in a workflow world

Our working day is an array of processes, procedures and workflows. It might start as soon as we swipe a security card through the door to the office, continue with completing an application for a corporate training course and end up with submitting a form to claim travel expenses. Some of these processes are automated. Whenever we send an e-mail a disclaimer appears at the end without any need to write it out every time. Most of the procedures are in place because of a need to satisfy compliance and regulatory requirements, especially with regard to any financial or personnel decision. Even quite a small organization will have a number of information technology (IT) systems, all of which are based around workflows and databases. Business analysts and developers may well have interviewed us and spent many months working out every possible workflow variation so that these applications can be successfully designed and implemented.

All these procedures and workflows capture data that somewhere along the line may be used to make a business decision. Often this decision is based on aggregated data, perhaps about employee costs or the number of calls to a Help Desk. In aggregating the data and placing it in context, information has been created. Hopefully, there are also processes in place to archive the information, completing an information life cycle that could be made up of many individual processes.

No matter how many systems are in place, and how many procedures are developed, they will never cover every eventuality. Most systems in organizations are designed to collect information, not to distribute it around the organization. When working for an organization with operations in even one other country the systems complexity is substantially increased. We may find an Excel spreadsheet of revenues by customer but is it in euros or sterling? Are they US dollars or Canadian dollars? Is the spreadsheet the latest version? Who can we call to check on the data in one of the cells?

The result is that there are a very large number of informal processes that are not supported by an IT system or even subject to compliance and regulatory oversight. An office may have moved its location, there is a new managing director at a subsidiary company, and the date of the office party has been changed. In any organization, every day there are changes and additions to the information that people depend on to carry out their work in a way that is both satisfying and contributes to the organization.

The answer, in any organization that has an intranet, is to publish all this information on the intranet, where it joins thousands of other items of information for which there is often no defined workflow, or process, but which could be important in some way to the effective operation of the organization. That is how intranets usually start and how, in most organizations, they continue to operate – just a very large notice board on which people place information notes in a range of formats, but never get around to taking them down when the information is no longer current or accurate. Someone gets the task of just keeping an eye on the intranet until the day comes that a senior manager relies on information on the intranet to make an important decision, and finds that the information is inaccurate. The call goes out to Human Resources (HR) to find an intranet manager.

The intranet opportunity

What is the value of an intranet to an organization? The first intranet management challenge is that it is all things to all people. To some it is a communications channel, to others a place to work with members of a team. It might offer employee self-service applications or ensure that the organization is compliant with industry and government regulations. The diversity of use is as wide as the diversity of users, and yet all are using the same intranet application.[1]

NetJMC's report *Global Intranet Trends 2009*[2] highlighted five features that were common to high-performance intranets. As a way of opening up discussions with senior directors and intranet managers about the value of an intranet, I adapted this approach and added a sixth feature, to come up with the schematic in Figure 1.1 of how an intranet adds value to an organization.

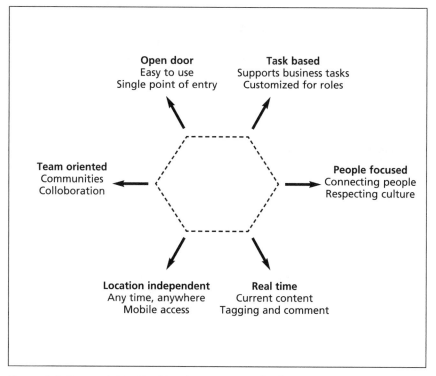

Figure 1.1 How an intranet adds value to an organization

In one global IT company I was working for, the corporate strategy had the following core elements:

- Empower people
- Work smart
- Innovate
- Customer first
- Create value.

Superimposing these values on the hexagon model resulted in Figure 1.2. This diagram immediately showed how the intranet was core to the achievement of corporate objectives and how investment in the intranet would have a substantial impact on the company.

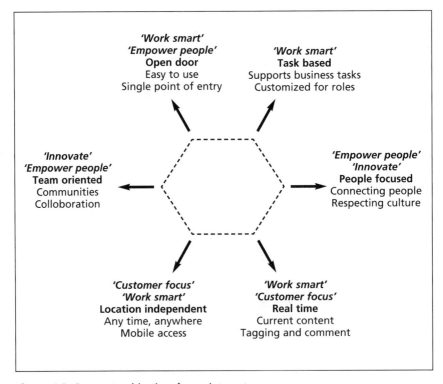

Figure 1.2 Corporate objectives for an intranet

Life as an intranet manager

I doubt that there will be a single reader of this book who set out on their career path determined to be an intranet manager. Intranet managers have a very diverse range of backgrounds, starting in IT, web design, librarianship, communications or marketing. Somewhere along the road they become involved in some way with the organization's intranet, perhaps as a content contributor for a department or subsidiary. Then the day arrives when the opportunity comes to take on the role of managing the intranet. Probably no other position gives someone the chance to be directly involved in all the business activities of the organization, providing an application that everyone with a desktop PC will probably see at the start of every working day and make use of throughout the day and throughout their career in the organization.

Official UK government statistics (Office for National Statistics) indicate that there were at least 50,000 intranets in businesses at the end of 2008[3] – and that would exclude many public sector organizations. So that means there are least 50,000 intranet managers, though few will have that title or have the intranet as their only responsibility. Many intranet managers are also responsible for other activities in their department, and find it difficult to prioritize their work when departmental work has to take precedence over the enterprise-wide responsibility for the intranet. It is likely that they will have seen the intranets of only a few other organizations, and will have only a limited idea of what can be achieved with an intranet, and what is regarded as good practice.

In most organizations the intranet is accessible to all employees working at a desk, and perhaps also to many employees working in manufacturing and customer-facing roles, through specialized terminals and kiosks. Other than e-mail and office productivity applications such as MS Office, it is probably the only application that is open to all employees, and so is a very 'high touch' application. The intranet home page may well be automatically loaded when the PC is switched on, so that there is not even the need to add a password or to click on an icon to open it. It is a pervasive application, and yet often receives minimal support, investment or governance.

There are two reasons for this benign attitude to the intranet. The first is that the organization does not appreciate that information is an asset. The other assets are all the responsibility of senior managers. HR looks after staff as an asset and Finance looks after the money, and may well take the lead on managing buildings and other physical facilities. IT may have a view that it is managing information, but the reality is that it is managing the technology infrastructure and not the content infrastructure. Not only is no one directly responsible for managing information as an asset, but this asset does not appear on the balance sheet.

The second reason is that the intranet is a stealth application. In the course of a working day perhaps 50% of employees may use the intranet to locate information or another employee. They have perhaps been online for only a few seconds, a period of time which would cause great anxiety to a web manager. In that few seconds on a well-designed and managed intranet the employee has found the information they need to move on in their task. They may then send an e-mail to someone they have identified in the staff directory, but it will almost certainly not start with 'I found you using the intranet'. In a large company perhaps tens of thousands of pieces of information are found each day using the intranet, and yet there is no visible trace of all this activity.

A key task for an intranet manager is to make the invisible transactions visible, and that is why Chapter 15, on measuring user satisfaction, is one of the longest chapters in this book.

The challenges of intranet management

In theory, intranet management should be very straightforward. It is about keeping information, technology and governance in balance (Figure 1.3):

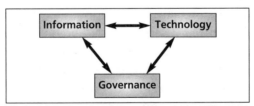

Figure 1.3 Keeping information, technology and governance in balance

Information

This needs to be of the highest possible quality and relevance to the business requirements of the organization. This requires a very clear view of what these requirements are. The moment the intranet becomes a dumping ground for anything that does not have a home in another enterprise system, and there are no quality standards, users will lose trust in the intranet and use other connections.

Governance

This should set out the objectives, standards, operational processes, resources and plans for the intranet. The issue here is keeping a balance between the mandatory (e.g. each page to have the name of the content contributor) and the advisory (e.g. in general, lists should be ordered in an alphabetical sequence). However, a mandatory requirement for which there is no 'penalty' for non-conformance just becomes advisory.

Technology

This sets out the way in which the technology will support access to the information, according to the principles set out in the governance framework. In practice, intranets are often technology driven, and here SharePoint is a good example of where the technology may not be appropriate to all intranet requirements. If, in the wider interests of the organization, SharePoint (or an IBM Web Sphere portal) is the default platform, then the governance processes have to take this into account, and the way in which information is published may have to be reviewed.

In practice, the situation is complicated by the range of stakeholders (Figure 1.4).

In the case of an intranet one of the unique challenges is that there are two user communities. There is the community of users who access the intranet to retrieve information, and there is the user community that contributes to the

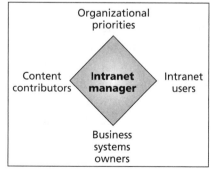

Figure 1.4 Intranet stakeholders

intranet. This is a critically important front-office/back-office relationship. In virtually all other IT-based applications content is added as part of the workflow; for example, submitting a purchase order, or applying for a new computer. This is usually not the case with an intranet, and the scale of content contribution is often invisible to all except the individual content contributors, who are rarely rewarded with even the recognition that their work is additional to all the other tasks they undertake for the organization.

Add in changing organizational priorities and the need to work closely with the IT and business owners of other systems, and it becomes obvious that the core skill of an intranet manager might well be as a negotiator, trying to move the intranet forward while balancing the interests of all the stakeholders.

A framework for intranet management

There is currently no professional certification for intranet managers. There are certainly many events with a workshop format, and a number of larger events that take place around the world each year. There are many intranet communities that seem to be growing rapidly in size and value. However, none of these events supports anything close to a structured course in intranet management. Intranet managers have to learn on the job, and only in very large organizations will there be other intranet managers to guide and mentor someone taking on this role for the first time.

The objective of this book is to provide a framework for the competencies that an intranet manager probably needs to have if they are to be able not just to cope with the challenges of managing the diverse and often divergent needs of stakeholders, but also to positively thrive on the opportunity they now have to make a substantial contribution to the development of the organization.

However, this is not intended to be primarily an academic textbook but a practical handbook for intranet managers at whatever stage of maturity they, or the intranet they are responsible for, have reached.

The book is divided into four parts:

Part 1 Foundations
1 Managing intranets: opportunities and challenges
2 Defining user requirements
3 Making a business case
4 Developing a content strategy
5 Enhancing collaboration

Part 2 Technology
6 Managing rechnology
7 Specifying and selecting software
8 Using Microsoft SharePoint for intranets

Part 3 Operational planning
9 Establishing the intranet team
10 Managing intranet projects
11 Evaluating risks
12 Conforming to compliance requirements
13 Enhancing the user experience
14 Marketing the intranet
15 Measuring user satisfaction

Part 4 Governance and strategy
16 Creating the governance framework
17 Developing an intranet strategy
18 From intranets to information management.

Arguably, intranet design should be part of this management framework, but that topic, as it deserves, now has a book in its own right: *Designing Intranets*, by James Robertson.[4]

Resource lists

At the end of each chapter there is a short list of websites and other resources that provide additional commentary and insight on the topics that have been covered. These resources can also be found at:

www.intranetfocus.com

where new and revised resources will also be listed.

Resources

1   Nielsen Norman Group: www.nngroup.com. Although perhaps better known for work on web usability, the Nielsen Norman Group has a significant intranet design and usability practice. *Intranet Design Annual* provides ten detailed profiles of intranets.

2   McConnell, J., *Global Intranet Trends*, http://netjmc.com. This report is published annually and provides a baseline into the way in which intranets are having an impact on the organization.

3   Office for National Statistics (2008) *Statistical Bulletin: E-Commerce and information and communication technology (ICT) activity 2008*.

4   Step Two Designs: www.steptwo.com.au. For over a decade James Robertson and his colleagues at Step Two Designs, an intranet consultancy based in Sydney, Australia, have published a wide range of reports on all aspects of intranet management. *Designing Intranets* was published in 2010.

2
Defining user requirements

Introduction

I have highlighted in Chapter 1 that although the intranet supports many processes that may have a workflow element its scope is not defined by processes in the same way as financial, HR, logistics and other applications. Because each employee assesses the value of a piece of information in a different way from any other employee in the organization, probably the most challenging issue for an intranet manager is defining the user requirements for the intranet, both currently and in the near future.

It is for this reason that this chapter on defining user requirements comes so early in the book. Everything else, from the selection of technology to the governance structure, and from the content strategy to performance evaluation, has to be based on user requirements. Just because all the users will be employees of the organization does not make the task any easier, because they will have very high expectations that the intranet will be of significant value to them.

This chapter focuses on techniques which are of value either in the case of the initial launch of an intranet, or when the need for a major programme of enhancement is identified from regular monitoring of the value and impact of the intranet, as described in Chapter 15. The chapter does not cover the translation of these user requirements into the design of the architecture of the intranet, a subject outside the scope of this book but covered in detail by James Robertson's *Designing Intranets*.[1]

The solution is personalization!

A number of organizations have taken the view that the ideal way to solve the problems of information overload and providing only what is relevant to an individual employee is to use portal technology to provide a personalized view of the information on an intranet. In theory this is an excellent idea, but in practice there are some fundamental problems:

- The information needs of an individual employee are highly specific to the knowledge, expertise and experience of that employee. To provide a personalized desktop requires a detailed understanding of this information requirement so that the appropriate portlets and personalization tools can be developed. This is very time consuming.
- Employees have multiple roles. A business development manager could also be a project manager on a project to relocate the office. In the course of the day they will flip between both these roles, and require the portal to do the same. In this particular example the project may only last a couple of months, and yet a specific view of a set of documents or applications will have to be developed.
- If an employee has to operate in a locked-down desktop situation then there are two dangers. The first is that they compare notes with a colleague performing the same task in a different country

and discover that they have different desktops. The second is that a degree of complacency will set in and the employee will forget that they do have some options available to them. In the case of one major international consulting business there were 90 different portlet options available, but screen space for only around ten.

The evidence suggests that personalization is used to only a very limited extent, and that its use does not seem to be increasing at the present time. There is a wider use of customization, where a small number of roles have been defined, such as Sales and Marketing, and either role-specific applications have then been developed or there are a number of different 'home pages' at the first level of the intranet architecture.

Microsoft Product Description Cards

In 2002 Microsoft user experience researchers Joey Benedek and Trish Miner developed a set of 118 adjectives that could be used to define usability in test situations.[2] These words include Difficult, Organized, Fun and Time-Consuming.

There are various ways of using these terms in the process of starting to define user requirements. Ideally, each word should be written on a card and a set of cards given to small groups of users. The number in each group should be no more than five, because the objective is to get a discussion going about the terms that best describe the current intranet and the terms that should define the relaunched intranet. Each group should be asked to select eight cards for the current intranet, and then in a second run (when everyone has had a chance to look at the complete deck) for the new intranet. Once eight have been selected, the groups might then be asked to bring the total down to five.

In analysing the results it can be of value to identify not only the common descriptive terms but also those that seem not to fit the pattern. Exploring why just one group chose the word 'Fun' can often result in a very useful conversation about user perceptions and requirements.

The set of words can also be used in a larger group with each individual first circling eight words, and then reducing the number down to five. This approach can work well when used as a short session within a more general management meeting, perhaps of sales managers or customer support engineers. The set of adjectives may well be different from those generated from group work but can be equally valuable in capturing expectations for the intranet.

The set of terms should be widely publicized, and then used as a baseline in the development process. To know that the common attributes that the groups chose were:

(In a legal practice)
- businesslike
- clean
- integrated
- organized
- professional,

as compared with:

(A UK children's charity)
- accessible
- appealing
- engaging
- friendly
- motivating

could assist significantly in developing the design of the intranet, and probably the home page.

Personas

A widely used technique in the design and development of websites and intranets is the use of personas[3]. A persona is a fictional person who represents characteristics of a group of people with similar requirements for information to undertake tasks.

Personas bring many overall user-focus benefits, including:

- Users' goals and needs become a common point of focus for the team.

- The team can concentrate on designing for a manageable set of personas, knowing that they represent the needs of many users.
- By always asking 'Would Anne use this?' the team can avoid the trap of building what users ask for, rather than what they will actually use.
- Design efforts can be prioritized based on the personas, and so design and project creep can be managed.
- Disagreements over design decisions can be sorted out by referring back to the personas.
- Designs can be constantly evaluated against the personas where appropriate, using business end users who were involved in the development of the persona.

More recently, personas have been applied to intranets, with excellent results. These are some specific benefits:

- Content is written in an appropriate style and structure for the persona.
- Decisions can be made on the requirements for personalized and customized information.
- Intranet content architectures can be optimized for specific personas so that there is a balance between search and browse.

However, the process of developing information applications that meet the requirements of a set of personas does not stop at the development of the personas themselves. Each persona has to be further developed so as to identify the tasks that the persona will perform and how they will use information in completing that task. These are often referred to as 'use cases'.[4]

In the case of an intranet there will almost certainly be more than one audience, and the question then needs to be addressed of how many personas should be developed. The answer is probably no more than four or five, though to reach that number the initial selection might be as high as eight to ten personas. It is very easy to let the process get more complicated and time consuming than it either needs or deserves to be.

The usability consultant Donald Norman sums it up well:

Do Personas have to be accurate? Do they require a large body of research? Not always, I conclude. The Personas must indeed reflect the target group for the design team, but for some purposes, that is sufficient. A Persona allows designers to bring their own life-long experience to bear on the problem, and because each Persona is a realistic individual person, the designers can focus upon features, behaviours, and expectations appropriate for this individual, allowing the designer to screen off from consideration all those other wonderful ideas they may have. If the other ideas are as useful and valuable as they might seem, the designer's challenge is to either create a scenario for the existing Persona where they makes sense, or to invent a new Persona where it is appropriate and then to justify inclusion of this new Persona by making the business case argument that the new Persona does indeed represent an important target population for the product.[5]

User interviews

It is important to consider carefully the choice of interviewee, and the duration and structure of the interviews that are essential in understanding the way that information is discovered and used in accomplishing a task. This is because it can be so easy to move away from the core subject of the interviews and get into specifics of design and content that are then difficult to scale up to a set of user requirements.

Box 2.1 outlines an approach to user interviews that has worked out well in consulting projects I have undertaken.

At first this may seem a lot of detail and process 'just for an interview', but you are taking up the time of the interviewee, and your own time, so it is best to make the most effective use of the 50 minutes. You also want the interviewee to feel that their views are important and that you are making every effort to ensure that you record these views.

Decision support

In many respects the intranet is a decision-support application. Over some years of conducting user-requirements interviews, I have found

Box 2.1 Conducting user interviews

1   Accept that through the interviews alone you will not reach a consensus on user requirements. Some may immediately come to the top of the list but others will not emerge until the initial designs for the intranet can be demonstrated.

2   Selecting whom to interview is a mixture of research and politics. There are some people who need to be interviewed because it is important that they feel part of the project, even though they may not be able to specify tasks with an adequate level of detail.

3   Plan the interview to last no more than 50 minutes. If this turns out not to be enough time, then make an appointment for a second interview.

4   Make sure that as far as possible all the interviewees know who is on the list. You will then get hyperlinks such as 'When you talk to George ask him to tell you about Project Aurora', which can be very useful.

5   Where possible, undertake the interview in the working space of the interviewee, who may then be able to demonstrate a situation or a resource that they use.

6   Prior to the interview set out on a single piece of paper your own background, the objectives of the interview and how the results will be used. You may not be known to the interviewee; a brief CV and the objectives, perhaps set out on a PowerPoint slide, significantly reduce the time taken to do the introductions. This can also be of value when you need to conduct an interview over the telephone or a video link.

7   Take time to research the background of the interviewee, for example, how long they have been in the organization and what different roles they have had. This information might come from HR, but it is better to ask the interviewee to provide a 100-word synopsis of their own background as they will almost certainly bias it to things that they want you to know, and that in itself is useful.

8   Emphasize that the interview is 'off the record' and that although you will be taking notes you will not attribute any opinions or information provided by the employee without their express permission.

9   Try to prepare some form of diagram that can be used in the interview, such as the one shown in Figure 1.1 (page 5). You will find that interviewees will start to write on their copy about aspects of their work. Just asking questions may well not prompt the same reaction.

Continued on next page

Box 2.1 (Continued)

10 Avoid asking what information the interviewee uses in their role. Most people use a very wide range of sources, and so almost from the beginning the discussion can start to stray away from the anticipated line of questioning.

11 Focus instead on what decisions the interviewee has to make, and how they find and use (and those are two different actions) the information they need. Another approach is to present them with a list of some typical tasks (see below).

12 Make sure that there is a clock that is visible to both you and the interviewee. If you use a watch, the interviewee will think that you are more anxious about the time than you are about what they are saying. They too can keep a track of the time, which is just as important to them as it is to you.

13 Make notes on a preformatted piece of paper that has boxes for items such as the name and contact details of the interviewee and also one specifically for people who are mentioned in the interview as being important to make contact with. The benefit of using sheets of paper rather than a notebook is that they can be sorted into multiple sequences, such as all those who mentioned HR self-service, or those who had an important requirement for external information. This is much more difficult to do when using a notebook.

14 About 30 minutes into the interview, summarize the initial outcomes of the meeting and agree the agenda for the next 10 minutes. This might be to go back over something in more detail, or to explore some items that have not yet been covered. It can also be interesting to find out the response to the question 'How would you evaluate the success of the intranet?'

15 At the 40-minute mark, start to bring things to a close and offer the interviewee your 'magic pen'. This is the pen you have been using but now you transfer authority to the interviewee by saying that while they are holding the pen anything that they really want to come true will do so. This final five minutes may seem contrived, but during this time the interviewee will feel empowered to move beyond their formal position and offer a vision of how the intranet could be of benefit to them and their colleagues.

16 Finally, summarize the outcomes, ticking each one off on the note sheet so that the interviewee can see that all their comments have been recorded. Emphasize the confidentiality of the interview and make sure that you have contact details so that, if necessary, you can ask further questions for clarification, and also send the interviewee a brief summary of the outcomes of the interview.

that a number of tasks come up with considerable regularity. Although interviewees are likely to focus on some of their common tasks, statements such as the following can sometimes draw attention to a more infrequent but very important task:

1 What work is the organization doing on [...]?
2 What has happened to this project/topic since [date]?
3 What other documents are there similar to this one?
4 Who can I ask for advice on [...]?
5 Who is this person?
6 I need to find the membership of this [group] to see if there is any one on it I know.
7 What have been the outcomes of this project/initiative?
8 What are the procedures for [...]?
9 What are the key documents on [...]?
10 Where can I find the document on [...]?
11 What has the organization done in similar situations to [...]?
12 What are the related documents to this one?
13 I need to find all the documents on this topic, for compliance reasons.
14 I need to see information from both external and internal sources on this topic.
15 I need to share information on [...] with my team.
16 I want to be alerted when new information on this topic is added to the system.
17 I want to restrict my query to a specific group of documents.
18 I need the definitive document on [...].
19 Who should be the members of a team to come up with a solution to this problem?
20 Which of our suppliers or customers might have a solution to this problem?

For each query, the user's actions can be explored with some follow-on questions:

• What prompts the need to undertake the query – were you asked by someone else, or is it part of your standard job profile to carry out this query every month [for example]?

- What resources do you use, and why?
- How confident are you that you have found all the relevant information?
- How confident are you that the information you have found can be trusted?
- What do you do with the information you have found?

Clearly, all of these questions cannot be accommodated in a 50-minute interview, but the list can often be reduced to a small number tailored to the nature of the work of the employee. It is much better to arrange a follow-up interview than to try to squeeze everything into just an hour.

Focus groups

Interview programmes will be time consuming, and take several weeks to complete and analyse. Usually, there is then pressure from senior managers to set up some focus groups. These rarely have the desired result, as the participants may be unwilling to highlight problems that they find in obtaining and using information, lest the other participants mark them down as incompetent. Running a focus group also requires two people, one to facilitate and one to record the comments, so some of the potential gains in interviewer time are already at risk. Then there is the challenge of making sure that all the participants turn up, so that the group is representative of a group of employees. Having someone miss the meeting and then insist on having an individual interview again wastes time and delays the conclusion of the project.

Focus groups tend to work well in the following situations:

- bringing together a group of new employees, who will welcome the chance to expand their networks
- having a group to explore a specific and well-defined issue, such as defining the requirements for a staff directory or enabling access to external information
- working with content contributors on how they would like to be

able to work with the intranet team
- discussing among a group of senior stakeholders, who know each other well, issues such as business-critical processes for the organization that need to be supported in the intranet
- bringing together employees who represent a common persona, to confirm or revise the tasks associated with that persona.

In all other cases, focus groups to determine user requirements will almost always end up being a waste of time and effort.

Seeing the complete picture

The process of developing a set of requirements needs to include good feedback to users and other stakeholders. As always with intranets, there will be trade-offs between the requirements of different sets of users, and these need to be reconciled (as far as is possible) at a fairly early stage in the process, and then again as the process moves nearer to the design phase. The more that the requirements can be converted to wireframes the better, as users think in 'web' terms, and the moment they see even a fairly rough layout of the home page or a sectional structure, more and often better ideas will be brought up.

In the final analysis it will not be possible to meet everyone's requirements, and this has to be made clear to all involved in the process. It should also be made clear that there will be continual monitoring of the intranet through the approaches set out later in Chapter 15, so that if a key requirement has slipped through the initial design net it can be implemented in due course.[6]

Resources

1   James Robertson has written *Designing Intranets: creating sites that work* (Step Two Designs, 2010), which goes into considerable detail about how to identify user requirements, www.steptwo.com.au.
2   Microsoft Corporation has published a number of papers on user requirements methodologies, including the Product Reaction Cards: www.microsoft.com/usability/UEPostings/ProductReactionCards.doc

www.microsoft.com/usability/uepostings/desirabilitytoolkit.doc

http://msdn.microsoft.com/en-us/testing/bb414765.aspx

http://msdn.microsoft.com/en-us/magazine/dd569755.aspx.

3   Steve Mulder, with Ziv Yaar, has written a very practical book on persona
     development, but there is little direct advice on intranet persona
     development:
     Mulder, S. and Yaar, Z. (2007) *The User Is Always Right*, Berkeley, CA: New
     Riders.

4   George Olsen has published a very detailed persona development
     methodology:
     www.interactionbydesign.com/presentations/olsen_persona_toolkit.pdf.

5   Don Norman is one of the founders of the Nielsen Norman Group, and
     his view on personas can be found at:
     www.jnd.org/dn.mss/adhoc_personas_em.html.

6   The Boxes and Arrows website is an excellent source of information on all
     aspects of defining a user experience:
     www.boxesandarrows.com.

3
Making a business case

Introduction

Any internal investment made by an organization will always need to be justified by a business case, especially in the current economic situation. Many organizations have a pro forma approach to investment cases that can be very difficult to adapt to the delivery of what, in essence, is an information service. This was the case with a major hospital in the UK where most of the investment was targeted at meeting performance targets for clinical excellence set out by the government. The entire pro forma was based around patient numbers and treatments and it was totally unsuitable for an investment into new web content management software for the intranet. There was general agreement at all levels in the hospital that the intranet was a valuable support tool, but the intranet manager was placed in the situation of not being able to show an auditable link between the investment and clinical performance – the alternative being to persuade the hospital trust that the investment pro forma needed to be rewritten.

In this chapter a number of different ways of making a business case for an intranet are presented, all of which will need to be adapted to the way in which investment decisions are made by the board. Indeed, the initial step has to be to establish any rules for investment decisions before starting to prepare the business case, especially where the investment is for computer hardware and software. There are often levels of investment that can be signed off by an individual senior manager without having to go to the finance director and the board. Sometimes it pays to be pragmatic and to pitch the investment at a level where it does not need full board approval, as almost always in the intranet business some investment is better than none at all.

The focus of this chapter is on making a near-term business case, perhaps for the next 6 to 12 months. Preparing a longer-term, perhaps three- or even five-year, strategy is covered in Chapter 17.

All or something?

One decision to be made at the outset is whether the best approach is to write a business case for the entire intranet or to take some specific elements of the intranet and use those to make such a good business case that everything else can be wrapped into it. One of the benefits of making a close study of the Intranet Innovation Awards, sponsored by Step Two Designs, is that they show very effectively that targeting action towards a specific group of employees or a specific task can result in sufficiently dramatic outcomes that it would be an immensely brave manager who then decided that the intranet was not a business-critical application.[1] The 2009 Award winner, AEP, a US-based electricity utility, created an online ideas system that identified $8 million in savings, $2 million in the first month alone. A similar approach at British Airways also identified some substantial savings and enhanced operational efficiencies that were a result of the intranet.

Identifying localized business-case opportunities cannot be achieved by sitting at the intranet manager's desk all day. Whether from the initial research into user requirements (Chapter 2) or the feedback from users (Chapter 15), it is essential that intranet managers maintain very good working relationships with as many groups and departments as possible and be open to ideas, even if they seem to be of value to only a small group of employees.

Defining business priorities

If a pitch is going to be made that the intranet is a business-critical application, then it follows that the intranet manager needs to be certain about what is critical to the business. Some examples are given Table 3.1.

This information can be provided only by someone at board level. It is unlikely even in a small organization that whoever the intranet

Table 3.1 The business-critical intranet	
Business objective	**Intranet investment justification**
Improve margins by keeping costs under control	Reduce travel costs through holding web meetings. Offer an ideas forum to identify cost savings and business efficiencies.
Expand through acquisition	Structure the intranet in a way that facilitates building transition intranet micro-sites, so as to reduce the induction period for a significant number of new employees coming on board at the same time. Pre-populate the staff directory with staff details from the acquired company so that synergies can be obtained.
Close business opportunities more effectively	Have a 'lessons learned' section where people can share information about past good bid decisions.
Avoid compliance breaches	Include compliance self-checking on the intranet so that staff have to complete a form or even a web-based examination to show that they have read and understood compliance requirements.
Make faster and better use of new employees, or employees changing their role and responsibility	The induction process is usually a nightmare for HR departments. A good induction section will enable a new member of staff to pace their own induction as needed. Effective use of social media will ensure that they are quickly part of established networks and can offer their experience and expertise. The requirements of employees changing roles and responsibilities, especially where relocation is involved, are often overlooked but can be just as challenging.
	Continued on next page

Table 3.1 (Continued)	
Business objective	**Intranet investment justification**
Facilitate acquisition and divestment	This is a scale-up of the employee induction scenario, but the visibility to stakeholders is very high. The board will be on the line to create added value very quickly and the intranet can be a very important enabler in making this happen. Equally important is managing divestment. It might make sense to have a plan for providing the acquiring company with a ready-made intranet for the division or subsidiary involved.
Make effective use of the workforce	The jury is probably still out on the value of expertise directories, but a well-designed staff directory can still be a very valuable asset for the business. Another aspect of workforce mobilization is the support of team working.
Strengthen the culture of the organization	On its own, an intranet cannot establish a culture, but as an internal communications application it can be very valuable in getting across core business requirements, such as a commitment to quality, high levels of customer satisfaction, and the maintenance of agreed ethical standards.
Be responsive to market changes	There can be a danger with an intranet that it provides only an internal view of the business. There are now many web-based news clippings services that can deliver targeted news to the intranet desktop, though these need to be complemented by a facility for staff to tag these news stories with comments of their own.
Focus on achieving business objectives	Many companies use techniques such as balanced scorecards and key performance indicators, but do not make this information widely available. The intranet is an excellent place to present this information, along with news stories about the organization, a list of major projects won and much else about the way in which the organization is seeking to achieve its targets in the current year.
Disaster management	The volcanic ash cloud in Europe in 2010 alerted many companies to the problems they faced if key workers were not able to participate in business meetings. The intranet can fulfil an important role by supporting remote access by staff to business-critical content.

manager reports to will be on the board, and they will therefore be unlikely to know in detail all the strategic thinking that the board has been engaged with. Having access to such information can thus put the intranet manager in the privileged position of knowing information that is not generally known to most of the other employees, an issue that also arises in the establishment of a governance framework.

It may require some creative thinking about how the 'information' element of a business priority is translated into an intranet objective, but it is essential that this work is undertaken. The closer the perceived fit of the intranet business plan to the corporate strategy, the more likely that resources and support will be made available.[2]

Risk management as a business case

One approach to identifying business requirements is to work through the corporate risk register. Every decision has a risk, and every failure to make a decision has a risk. That is why risk management in an organization can provide a substantial number of business-value case studies to use in a business case.[3,4]

At the core of risk management is a means of quantifying the risk. A risk (e.g. the intranet manager leaving) is scored on Impact × Probability, though there are some inherent problems with this approach.

Of these two parameters, probability is much more difficult to assess objectively, so concern is normally focused on risks that have a high impact, because whenever they occur the organization will be put at risk. Working through these risks may well identify an issue where the intranet can play an important role.

In one retail company there was considerable concern about a very aggressive new competitor. The intranet manager constructed a simple web application where staff could note particular lines that were on sale in the shops, references to the competitor in papers and magazines that they read, and the comments made by friends and neighbours. Although anecdotal and not very rigorous, a significant amount of competitive information was obtained at no cost to the company and, in addition, employees felt directly engaged in the process of responding to the challenge.

The reason why risk management can be a strong potential base for an intranet business plan is that corporate governance requires the directors of an organization to identify and manage risks to the business in a way that reduces the risks to stakeholders and shareholders. Risks are therefore on the board agenda, and someone in the organization has the responsibility of presenting these risks and maintaining a risk register. It can be difficult to identify the risk manager because, like many intranet managers, they do not have a formal title, but the financial, legal or internal audit departments are good places to start.

In the case of companies that make filings to the Security and Exchange Commission in the USA, the annual SEC 10K filing lists business risks in some considerable detail in Section 1A. To give an example, the risk headings used by Pfizer in the SEC 10K filing dated 26 February 2010 are:

- Health care reform
- Government regulation and managed care trends
- Generic competition
- Competitive products
- Dependence on key in-line products
- Specialty pharmaceuticals
- Research and development investment
- Development, regulatory approval and marketing of products
- Post-approval data
- Biotechnology products
- Research studies
- Interest rate and foreign exchange risk
- Risks affecting international operations
- Diversified segment
- Global economic conditions
- Difficulties with our wholesale distributors
- Product manufacturing and marketing risks
- Cost and expense control/unusual events
- Changes in laws and accounting standards
- Terrorist activity
- Legal proceedings
- Business development activities
- Information technology
- Failure to realize all of the anticipated benefits of the acquisition of Wyeth.

It would be surprising if, in most of these sections, there was not some role for the intranet to be able to provide access to information and knowledge that would enhance the ability of Pfizer to manage these risks.

Productivity as a business case

Intranet discussion lists invariably contain a plea from an intranet manager requesting advice on how to make a business case for an intranet on the basis of a return on the investment (ROI) or on enhancements to productivity. James Robertson, from Step Two Designs, has set out 25 reasons why business cases based on productivity do not work.[5,6] These are set out in Table 3.2. In the introduction to the blog posting, Robertson stated:

> The problem is that productivity metrics are fatally flawed, in almost every respect. They are a bad basis for intranet teams to justify their existence or demonstrate their value, and are dangerous in ways that aren't properly recognized. So as a service to intranet teams, I'd like see if I can demolish this once and for all.

The list is quoted in full, as, time and time again, intranet managers are asked to provide an ROI for an intranet. It should not and cannot be done.

Table 3.2 Intranets and productivity justifications	
Issue	Justification
We're not measuring end-to-end task completion	This metric focuses solely on the time needed to find information on the intranet, not the task or activity itself. When establishing a new customer credit card, how much of that time is spent on the intranet, versus working in the front-line systems? Much more valid productivity gains can be argued from improving end-to-end performance, not just 'finding stuff'.
Can we realize the value?	In financial jargon, financial benefits must be 'realized', before they count. In other words, if we save $1.7 million, can we get this as cash or equivalent? In practice, there are only two real ways of concretely realizing the benefits: increase the number of tasks that can be done by the same number of staff, or reduce head count (sack people). As intranet teams, we're rarely in a position to use either of these approaches (and maybe wouldn't want to).
Time saving and productivity is complex	So we've saved each staff member 2 minutes a day, do they now spend all that time in productive ways? Or do they spend it reading the newspaper or chatting on Facebook? Some while back I read research on how different types of staff make use of time savings, and it highlighted big differences between blue collar, white collar and senior managers. Our calculations make a lot of assumptions and simplifications. (I now can't find this research, can anyone help?)
	Continued on next page

Table 3.2 (Continued)	
Issue	**Justification**
We are multiplying a lot of assumptions	How valid is a figure when we have to make a dozen different assumptions, and then multiply them all together? The more we look at the calculations, the more the details squirm in our fingers. At their most extreme, the numbers obtained are simply wacky.
Many financial people won't accept it	In many organizations, CFOs and their staff simply won't accept these types of metrics, for the intranet or any other system. Better check first!
It's only about usability	Measuring time spent on the intranet is easy, but not very relevant. Why are we not demonstrating actual business benefits, rather than just improved findability?
How many staff are using the intranet?	We comfortably multiply out the time saved by the number of staff in the organization, but this seems somewhat optimistic. How many staff are actually using the intranet? In many cases, the problems with the intranet mean that few are using it, and so the nominal benefits will be small.
Increasing usage now costs us money	We've made the argument that reducing time spent on the intranet will save the organization, yet simultaneously we are aiming to increase intranet adoption. By this argument, the greater the number of intranet users, the more money we lose. We can't have it both ways.
Tell me again, are we trying to increase or decrease usage?	One of the most common metrics of intranet success is usage: visits, pages and hits. On the other hand, we're trying to demonstrate a reduction in time spent on the intranet, and the number of pages visited per task. Pick one.
The intranet is considered in isolation	The intranet sits alongside (and competes with) every other way of completing a task or getting an answer. This includes asking the person next to you, ringing someone up, or using a bit of paper. To make our calculations valid, we have to assume that the intranet is the only source of information, which may be the case in some situations, but certainly not universally.
We don't consider experience	Experienced staff just know how things work, as well as the answers to common questions and issues. They don't need to look up the intranet. So reliance on the intranet will naturally change over the lifetime of a staff member, but this is not factored in.
What about learnability?	No matter how bad an intranet is, given enough time, staff will often learn how to use what they need (or will give up entirely). This is not considered in the comparative usability studies.
How often are these tasks done?	Savings are generally calculated based on the before-and-after testing of a number of 'common' tasks on the intranet, such as looking up a phone number, or applying for leave. How often does an individual staff member actually do these tasks? In the case of applying for leave, it may only be once or twice per year, certainly not daily.

Continued on next page

Table 3.2 (Continued)	
Issue	Justification
Are the usability testing results valid?	To determine time savings, quantitative usability testing is required, which obviously can't be done at the same time as qualitative testing. Even when run carefully, it is widely recognized that usability testing is somewhat artificial, with user behaviour different from that in the real world (would we really spend 15 minutes looking for the leave form, or would we be on the phone asking for help within 2 minutes?).
Are we testing the right tasks?	In order to be relevant across a wide range of staff, tests tend to focus on general intranet activities. These generic tasks often relate to the staff directory, HR, finance, news, etc. Most are 'corporate services' activities that are not directly related to the day-to-day business of staff, making them much less valuable and relevant.
Can we generalize out to the whole intranet?	We've tested a few 'representative' tasks, and have found before-and-after time savings. But this is just for 6–12 tasks; can this be generalized out to time savings across the whole intranet? This is a big leap to make.
All staff are assumed to be the same	The information needed by someone in HR is not the same as someone in Finance, the call centre, or out in the sales team. That makes it impossible to apply a single set of results and metrics to the organization as a whole.
What are we actually testing?	A typical task may be to find out how to apply for leave. Should that be a quick or slow task? Do we want people to carefully read the policy (perhaps), or are we just measuring the time taken to find it? User intention varies so greatly between tasks that simply aiming to reduce the time taken is simplistic.
We oversell the value of these metrics	I'm completely fine with using before-and-after usability testing to show that improvements have been made, and to demonstrate progress. As indicative findings, they have great value. But many organizations go way beyond this, claiming millions of dollars of savings and 100% 'performance improvements'. This is overstretch, and dangerous territory.
We are treating our managers as fools	The many numbers involved in justifying time savings smacks of 'blinding with science'. It all seems very plausible and detailed, until you look a little closer. In taking this approach, we risk treating our managers and stakeholders as fools, selling them vague figures as concrete business cases. If they call our bluff, we're in a lot of trouble.
At their most extreme, these approaches make us look like idiots	I'm sorry, improving intranet usability will save the world economy trillions of dollars? Even assuming this is said half in jest (and I'm not sure it is), this makes us look pretty foolish, and does nothing to build our reputation with business managers or other professionals.
	Continued on next page

Table 3.2 (Continued)	
Issue	Justification
Show me the real figures	A lot of what is published is hypothetical: 'We could save $3 million a year in an organization with 10,000 staff.' Theory is good, but show me the actual case studies with realities rather than assumptions. There are a few examples, but nowhere near enough to demonstrate that the theory can reliably be put into practice.
Negative business cases are dangerous	Once we start down the road of negative business cases based on money saved, we can get ourselves in a lot of trouble. What if the cost of all the intranet authors is measured, wouldn't it be a cost saving to reduce the number of writers? How do we justify an expensive new project, if we've started talking about costs? Wouldn't the quickest and easiest way to save money be to sack the intranet team and fully devolve intranet management? We always recommend intranet teams focus on positive business cases (increased capability or capacity) wherever possible.
We are setting ourselves up for failure	Using these types of metrics can rush us into quoting substantial productivity benefits, even as we are trying to fix the basics of the intranet. It's better to wait until the intranet is delivering direct business benefits before claiming such successes.
It doesn't give us a roadmap for future development	Once we improve usability, what then? The narrow focus on usability rather than functionality leaves intranet teams constantly tuning their existing sites, rather than looking for ways to deliver new business value.

It can also be of interest, when faced with a demand for an ROI/productivity business-case justification, to ask the chief financial officer (CFO) if they can provide some examples from other business cases for software investment 'so that we can get the format right'. Even where such business cases have been developed usually the assumptions are so vague or unsubstantiated that it is in fact very easy to make a comparable business case for an intranet on the same basis. Then the CFO has the problem, and not the intranet manager.

Business case sponsors

Much is made of the value of having a sponsor for the intranet. To a large extent, the purpose of linking the intranet into the business planning framework of the organization is to reduce the need for the sponsor to engage in special pleading for the intranet because it is seen as being a core business platform.

Sponsors can be of value at a business unit level, perhaps even more so than at a corporate level. An intranet may end up being justified by a number of different business cases from a range of departments, divisions or subsidiaries. For each of these business cases, having someone who is willing to go on the record about the benefit they and their colleagues will gain from the investment can be of significant value.

All organizations have to share out investment funds among a range of projects all competing for attention. Intranet managers can sometimes fail to realize this basic fact. It is usually fairly easy to find out what the other major investment cases will be for the coming financial year, and working with the people responsible for these business cases can often result in some useful synergies and a willingness to act as a business case sponsor for the intranet.

Aligning performance metrics and the business case

An important feature of any business case is how the ROI is going to be measured. Chapter 15 sets out many different approaches to measuring value and impact, and these need to be included in the business plan so as to give comfort to the senior managers responsible for signing off on the plan that the proposed benefits will be forthcoming and visible. If a benefit cannot be assessed, even if only in some indirect ways, then there is really no point in that benefit being used as a business case.

Business case development is not a linear process, but proceeds in an iterative fashion. If there is no apparent alignment of performance metrics and the business case for support and investment, then the process needs to start all over again. Sometimes the justification for not writing a business case, or for writing one without any metrics, is that the intranet sponsor will be able to sell the intranet to the board. That may be a good option, so long as the intranet sponsor retains their position and their credibility. If they move on or out, then the position of the intranet can suddenly be very uncertain. If there is a lack of senior management commitment, then there is no point in taking up the position of intranet manager.

The very fact that the organization has an intranet means that someone, at some time, was an intranet evangelist. Now, in the cold light of post-recession (hopefully!) economic conditions the intranet will probably come under increasing scrutiny, just at a time when the organization needs the best possible access to information and knowledge to meet its objectives. The success of any intranet strategy, and of the intranet itself, almost certainly lies in the extent to which its value and impact can be assessed by those who may not use it on a regular basis.

Getting to 'Yes'

Given the nature of the career development paths of intranet managers, few will have any previous experience of writing a business plan. Of course every company will have 'templates' for business plans, but for readers who have not had the pleasure of writing a business plan before, here are some suggestions for how to go about it, based on my experience of writing many such plans for clients over the last ten years (see Box 3.1).

Thinking ahead

As an intranet manager, it is unlikely that you will get much warning of the need to develop or revise a business case. News of an acquisition, divestment or organizational restructuring is unlikely to be shared with the intranet team ahead of time, even though that should be the case. One major European company spent several months towards the end of 2009 developing a five-year plan for the global intranet, serving around 80,000 employees in over 100 countries. The global intranet was based on a federation of around 30 large country intranets and four intranets managed by the main lines of business. Early in 2010 a new chief executive officer (CEO) was appointed, and within a couple of months a new regional structure was announced which integrated the business units into groups of merged country units. No account was taken of potential changes in user requirements or of the complexity of the changes needed in the structure of the intranet and the likely impact on usability and trust as this was undertaken.

Life is like that in any organization, not just large international

Box 3.1 Writing a business plan

1 Write the first version in PowerPoint, using no more than ten slides and nothing smaller than 14pt letters. Some day you may have to present the case, so you might as well get the PowerPoint ready! More important, it will help you focus on the key messages that you need to get across. Update the PowerPoint as you develop the business plan, but try to keep to ten slides, or thereabout.

2 Spend at least 15% of the time you have available in writing the executive summary. It may well be the most important 500 words you write in the next three years. Every word has to be used effectively. Get several other people to read it through who have no direct relationship to the intranet team but who will benefit if the plan is approved.

3 Have a look at the business plans that were developed for other enterprise applications. You may find that they are no more than memos! If you are then challenged as to why you left out staff costs, you may wish to comment that the business plan for the new help desk software did not include them either.

4 No one will be interested in what you have done, only in what you will do. A long history of the evolution of the intranet is not going to help your cause.

5 The more you can show that you will be able to measure value and impact, the less senior managers will feel that there is an unquantifiable risk.

6 Even if the business plan is going to the chief information officer (CIO) it is advisable to keep it technology light, with perhaps an appendix to deal with exactly what a new search application will do for the business.

7 Don't use embedded hyperlinks. The business plans may be read on a train, a plane or in the back of a taxi, none of which currently facilitates getting on to the internet.

8 Do use Google as an example, because whatever websites senior managers use, love or hate, you can be sure that they will think that Google sets the gold standard.

9 Try to include stories about how the intranet made a difference to the organization, or how, through not having content on the intranet, an opportunity was lost. If you don't have stories like this your chances of persuading senior managers that they should support your cause may be severely limited.

10 Frightening senior managers with the investment made by competitors rarely works. Unlike a website, they cannot see it for themselves.

11 Make it very clear that you understand the challenges, opportunities and risks that the organization faces.

12 Don't put a fall-back position into the business plan, but do develop one in any case.

companies. Intranet managers would be well advised to maintain the business plan on perhaps a quarterly update cycle, based on the feedback from users (Chapter 15) and potential changes to IT platforms (Chapter 6). Be alert to:

- changes in the senior management team, even if it is just a change in responsibility
- changes in market conditions, both positive and negative, that might result in business restructuring, acquisition or divestment
- changes in the IT strategy, such as outsourcing or the adoption of Software as a Service or cloud computing applications (see Chapter 6), which could have an impact on the intranet technology platforms
- changes in the strategy of a vendor, which may catalyse the need to evaluate other content management systems (CMSs), search or social media applications (see Chapter 7)
- changes in the compliance regime under which the organization operates.

Taking just a few minutes at a meeting of the intranet team to play 'what if' scenarios can be very valuable. For example, how will the following objections be dealt with:

- 'We've never spent any money on the intranet in the past. Why now?'
- 'You are exaggerating the risks we face by not making the investment'
- 'I doubt any of our competitors makes this level of investment'
- 'Next year possibly, but we have other priorities this year'
- 'I only rarely ever use the intranet'
- 'You are implying that we've made the wrong decisions in the past'
- 'If the intranet has been so poor how come our business is doing OK?'
- 'What evidence do you have that this investment will make any difference to our business performance?'

Resources

1 Step Two Designs sponsors the annual Intranet Innovation Awards and the descriptions of these awards often contain good illustrations of how to prepare a successful business case: www.steptwo.com.au/iia.

2 The Nielsen Norman reports *Intranet Design Annual* are also a source of business case ideas: www.nngroup.com/reports/intranet/design/.

3 A series of excellent papers on risk management methodologies and the value of using risk management can be found in a special issue of the *IBM Journal of Research and Development*, **54** (3) (2010), entitled 'Business Integrity and Risk Management'.

4 Hopkin, P. (2010) *Fundamentals of Risk Management*, London: Kogan Page, www.koganpage.com.

5 The analysis by James Robertson on why a productivity-based approach to business case development is invariably unsuccessful can be found at: www.steptwo.com.au/columntwo/25-reasons-why-saving-time-on-your-intranet-is-a-bad-metric/.

6 James Robertson has also written a guide to intranet development, *What Every Intranet Team Should Know*: www.steptwo.com.au/products/everyteam.

4
Developing a content strategy

Introduction

All too frequently content contribution to an intranet is best described as a 'hobby'. Content is added as and when there are no other jobs that have a higher priority, by employees who have ended up with the task by default. There are usually no standards for content contribution, limited training and no rewards. Is it any wonder that one of the most frequent criticisms of an intranet is that there are too many out-of-date pages and a lot of duplication? An intranet can only ever be as good as the content that it contains, so developing a content strategy and making sure that it is complied with is the best single way of enhancing the value of an intranet.

There is a lot of investment in information creation in an organization. In the 21st century virtually every employee is an information creator, even if that information is a quality check on a product before shipment. That quality check gets aggregated into the quality-management process and may well end up in a business intelligence application which is being accessed through the intranet. The salary bill of the company will approximate more or less to the investment being made in information creation. That is a very considerable amount of money, and the reason why an information management strategy is so important for any organization.[1]

Less is more

Few intranet managers are able to state with any confidence just how many pages of content the intranet contains, but there are highly likely to be some 80/20 rules in operation, along the lines of:

- Only 80% of the content has any value, but no one knows which 80%.
- 20% of the content is dangerous, as it is out of date or inaccurate, but no one knows which 20%.
- 80% of the people who are supposed to own content on the intranet now have different jobs with different responsibilities, or have left the organization, but no one knows who they are.

Those may seem some very depressing figures, but in many cases the truth is even more depressing. There are many stories about organizations that were migrating from one web content management system (WCMS) to another, and in the process went through all the content and marked up what could be excluded. The general rule is that the total number of pages of content that can be removed, or not migrated, is usually in the 20–25% range.

These situations arise from two causes. First, the staffing of the intranet is inadequate to police all the content that is added and also to remove content that has no value. Second, the intranet has no clear purpose and so becomes a dumping ground for content on the basis that it might be useful and, now that the department has added it to the intranet, it is someone else's problem to look after it.

Keeping a balance between what is useful and what has negligible value is not easy, and that is why having a content strategy is so important.

Focusing on tasks

Good intranets have a total user-requirements focus, as has been recommended in Chapter 3. A content strategy has to be rooted in what users need, and not what the organization thinks might be useful to them. This is why a content strategy based around tasks and processes is so important, both for the content itself and for the metadata used to provide context to the content and to support discovery through search or the information architecture. That does not mean to say that every piece of content should be task based, but anything that is not is going to need a specific justification for being on the intranet – and for clogging up the search engine.

This is where the personas come into play, but it would be surprising if all the business tasks had been included in what will usually be a set of core personas, and not an attempt to define all the users of an intranet. The priorities are typically going to be:

- content that results directly in revenue generation
- content that is needed for compliance and regulatory purposes
- content that defines corporate values, procedures and principles
- content that supports career development
- content that represents the information that employees need in order to manage the risks to business performance.

This is not a definitive list, but these all demonstrate the principle that the more the intranet provides information that makes people feel empowered, the more it will be respected, supported and used.

Information use cases

A useful way of looking at content management issues is to consider the triangle of use cases illustrated in Figure 4.1.

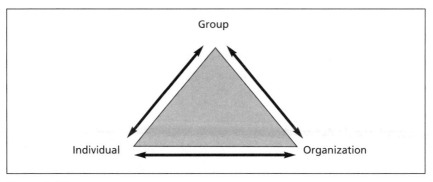

Figure 4.1 Intranet content user

- **Organization to individual** – In this category comes news about the organization and, of course, corporate policies and procedures.
- **Organization to group** – This group could be anything from a small team to a department or division. It is a group of people with specific interests, and so could be a group comprising all senior managers to whom HR wishes to send out information on potential redundancies.
- **Group to individual** – This could be information on the outcomes from a project team working a new quality standard, asking for comments on a draft.
- **Individual to organization** – Arguably, the staff directory could be an example of this use case, where each individual is responsible for their own record, but collectively this is of value to the entire organization.
- **Individual to group** – A group is composed of individuals, and this path could be a blog that a group of employees with a common interest subscribe to.

This is just one approach to looking at the granularity of information. All too often the approach is taken of publishing to an intranet every piece of content possible, and then putting the responsibility on to the users to find the information they need. The value of an intranet is directly related to the relevance of the information it contains and the trust that each employee can place in the quality of that information.

Information stewardship

At the heart of the matter is the concept of information stewardship, a concept that is rarely discussed at intranet conferences. In the context of this section, the term 'The Document' is used for any item of information. It could be a map or an organizational chart as well as a Word document.

If employees are unwilling to spend the time to maintain their personal profile, then spending even more time on content administration is not going to happen. One of the problems with intranets is that there are multiple stakeholders. The stakeholders are:

1   The manager to whom the content author reports and who has given implicit or explicit support to staff with content-contribution roles.
2   The content author who has written, often with the help of others, The Document.
3   The intranet page owner who writes and/or edits the HTML content which will act as a navigation page to The Document or a header to The Document.
4   The intranet publisher who adds The Document to the intranet, and who may need to revise an A–Z listing, or similar.
5   The content reviewer who provides a quality check, making sure that The Document is fit for purpose.
6   The intranet manager who notes that it has been added or has received a notification that it will be added.

Now, although there are six roles, they could be performed by anywhere between one and six people. Increasingly, the days of the content reviewer are numbered. CMS vendors are all very proud of their content review workflow processes, but in an intranet environment no one has the time to work through a batch of e-mails in their inbox each morning so as not to get a yellow card for not playing the game. There might be some compliance situations where review is important, but they are the exception rather than the rule.

As more and more user-generated content populates an intranet, for example from a SharePoint collaboration application or from a blog, the formal management of content is going to become much more informal, especially as content management applications make it much easier to publish content through a wizard-like interface.

The end result will be that the only people who matter in this process are the content author, the manager and the intranet manager, and this leads into a discussion about information stewardship. Information stewardship is about taking responsibility for a piece of content that has been added to the intranet. This content needs life-cycle management (Box 4.1).

> **Box 4.1** The three essentials of content life-cycle management
>
> - It has to be kept under review to make sure that it remains accurate, and a revised version is published if needed.
> - It has to have good metadata added to it, and this will need to be reassessed from time to time.
> - When it no longer has any value it needs to be either deleted, or archived as a business record.

Often the problem is that once the content creator has published The Document there is no incentive for them to continue to maintain it. One of the roles of the manager should be to ensure that content creation is included in the job descriptions of their staff, and that content creation and ongoing management are given appropriate levels of priority among the various other tasks that the content creator needs to perform. There are two challenges here. The first is that the department concerned may not be aware of the use that is being made of the content across the organization. The second is that in most companies around 10% of the staff leave each year.

When a content creator changes role in any way it should be the duty and responsibility of their manager to appoint someone else to manage the content. In most situations this should not be too much of a challenge. In many companies corporate documents have version control records and it would be the work of a few moments for the incoming content steward to revise the record with their name and change the metadata record to reflect the change. One of the benefits of this process is that the incoming member of staff has to become familiar with all the documents that could be of value to them in their new role.

The common response to this is that there is no need to take this approach, as the department owns the content. In an organizational construct that may be the case, but that also means that everyone thinks that it is someone else's job to look after the document. Departments also have limited lives, often less than the tenure of employees, and in that case, who now is the owner of the document?

It is important to define who the current owner of the document is. People are often looking for knowledge, not information. Finding a document about a method of managing the signal-to-noise ratio on a spectrometer might help someone to locate expertise on circuit design and optimization that could be of value in a problem being experienced with a heart-rate monitor. With the information stewardship approach, there is at least a chance of finding someone with the expertise, who may now be in a different department but is still listed as the document author. One solution to the problem of information stewardship is for ownership of the document to go with the content author to their new department.

There will also be cases where there is no natural steward. Then the intranet manager has to become involved and decide whether the content is of value to the organization (and this is where search and weblogs can be of some value), or whether it should be archived or deleted. If no one can be found who has a sufficient interest in the subject to take on the role, it seems very probable that the document has reached the end of its useful life.

Content review and the role of content protocols

CMS vendors are always keen to demonstrate the way in which content items can be subject to review by a more senior manager, and during demonstrations of the software these senior managers can usually be seen nodding in approval when the vendor demonstrates how an e-mail message or alert message can be sent to their desktop every time one of their team wishes to upload a new piece of content. Until the system is installed, these managers have no idea of the number of alerts that are going to arrive for their attention each day, if not each hour. Yet these same managers do not check on the e-mails that these same employees are sending out each day, often to people outside the organization.

Extensive workflow review regimes (and I use the word deliberately) do not work for intranets. They become a barrier to the immediate publishing of information that could be of value to any number of people in the organization, and cause immense frustration on the part of content authors. What invariably happens is that just in order to clear their in-box, the manager just clicks the 'Yes' box without even looking at the content.

The default approach should be that content is subject not to managerial review, but to peer review throughout the organization. If each content item is visibly owned by a member of staff, then they will soon receive comments about poor formatting, or the careless insertion of links, especially if the organization has implemented a 'comment' facility on each item of content. If the organization does not trust its employees to publish responsibly, then it faces issues of corporate responsibility and respect that are beyond the capability of any technology to remedy.

There may well be certain items of content, mainly related to compliance issues, that need to be authorized, but only to the extent that the content would have been authorized in a workflow world. If there is a concern that content contributors may cause havoc to the structure of the intranet, that should be addressed at the outset by training, with the opportunity for contributors to use a sand-box as a trial area before going live to the intranet.

The process of ensuring that there is a personal commitment to content quality can be addressed by content protocols. A protocol is a way of doing something. As an example, senior management may wish to approve what an employee wishes to enter in a staff directory as their expertise or a list of projects they have worked on. That is just too time consuming. The alternative is a content protocol that reads:

> Please take care when adding information to your staff profile. If you are not sure about the information you wish to add please discuss it with your line manager in advance. From time to time checks will be made on the

information in the directory. If you add content that is misleading or that you know to be incorrect, then this could result in disciplinary measures being taken.

I have found that the use of the word 'protocol' is more neutral and flexible than 'standards and guidelines'.

Records management

The linkage between an intranet and the records management function of an organization tends to be somewhat limited. The view is taken that the content author has defined the content as being a business record and so there is some mysterious parallel universe where all corporate documents go at the end of their life. There are many problems with this approach. The document may have reached the end of its life as a document of value to the intranet, but it may still have a significant compliance life remaining, perhaps for a further seven years or more. The next issue is that the document still needs to be seen in the context of the intranet. Indeed the document may be of compliance value, but does the HTML header indicate that all staff must read the document, and is there any mechanism for identifying who has read (or at least opened) the document?

This situation becomes even more complex across borders, and the requirements in Europe may be very different from those in the USA. Any content strategy has to take account of records management requirements, even if there is no formal records management department. Usually the legal department will take a keen interest in what might need to be deleted, especially where freedom of information legislation is in operation.

Metadata

The missing link in content strategies is usually metadata management. Sometimes the view is taken that it does not matter because the search application (especially if it offers semantic search) does not need metadata to be effective. This is not the case. Semantic search can be very valuable in many instances, but not in all, and all too few organizations run test queries against test collections when selecting an enterprise search application – but that is a subject for another book.

The challenge of adding metadata is that, usually, the person who wrote the document is the person least equipped to add metadata. They will always have difficulty in seeing things through other people's eyes. This is especially the case where concepts such as 'business plan', 'product design' and 'strategic plan', are involved and the document itself may not explicitly use those terms. Web content management vendors opt out of the challenge by providing a text box to which authors can add keywords. Unless there is control on the terms, even something as basic as a consistent way of describing companies and departments, the value of the metadata will be minimal.

Going to the other extreme and building a corporate taxonomy may well not be the answer, if only because of the very considerable resources that are needed not only to build a taxonomy but also to maintain it. Somewhere in between is the sweet spot. Lists of controlled terms, perhaps for areas of operation, can be very valuable. Just which countries constitute the area called 'South East Asia', for example?

This book is not about how to devise corporate taxonomy and metadata schedules, but it does encourage the intranet team to look with care at keeping a balance between good-quality metadata with a long shelf life, the training needed to ensure consistent application of that metadata, and the need for the content author to have time to consider what the optimum collection of metadata terms might be.

There are also some good practices in document management that should be adopted. Ideally, any page in any document should have a unique set of header and footer information, so that the origin of the document can be established by looking at any page. That requires there to be some standards, not just guidelines, on the use of headers and footers, version record boxes and informative titles. Report titles such as 'Project Hercules – Status and Next Steps' do not help readers or searchers. Changing the title to 'Annual Report on Environmental Audit Results 2009' helps a great deal, as will an executive summary that is a good reflection of the content and conclusions of the report, and not just an opinion piece about all the issues the author did not cover in the report but which, on reflection, they feel could be of interest.

Content review timelines

It is not uncommon to find a document on a corporate intranet that is dated 2007 or 2008. The concern on the part of the user will be whether this is the current version of the document. There are three elements of the content management strategy that need to come into play here:

- Every document is owned by an individual member of staff and their contact details will be included in the metadata associated with the document.
- There is a document review cycle that, at a minimum, ensures that every document is reviewed no later than 12 months after addition to the intranet, and from then on every six months. This is, of course, a lot of work, but if employees are given the responsibility of adding their own content and being responsible for it within the terms of their job description, then this is usually not an insuperable challenge.
- When a document has a defined compliance or business process role (such as recording the basis on which maternity and paternity leave is calculated), then there is a requirement not only to update the document within a given period of sign-off (say one week), but also to ensure that any linked documents are amended to indicate the existence of the new document.

Content management training

Compared with a corporate website, many more people will be contributing to the intranet not only through a CMS but by writing documents that are then accessed via the intranet, as well as through a range of collaboration and social media applications. All content contributors will need some guidance on how to write for the intranet, which in principle is the same as how to write for the web – but with some differences. One of these is to remember that in an international company there is a wide range of language skills, which could have an impact on both content contribution and content comprehension. Nowhere is this more apparent than in PowerPoint slide presentations, where the words on the slide seemed to be chosen to give the author the maximum amount of flexibility in deciding after the event what they actually said.

More important is training in the use of the content management application. Many organizations are now implementing a structured and certified training scheme for content contribution. Working on the basis that everyone can contribute to the intranet and problems will be picked up at the review stage of the content contribution workflow does not work. There is just not enough time to review every item of content, and most people get quite upset when told that their approach is not correct. All too often workflow actually becomes workstop.

At the heart of the matter is gaining organizational recognition that content contribution should be a component of the job description. Once that has been achieved, then staff can be trained on procedures that are important for achieving their personal objectives. Very little has been written about good practice in content management training, which, given the highly distributed content authoring model of an intranet, is somewhat surprising.

A good place to start is to create some content publishing personas as a means of segmenting the training needs of the organization, as illustrated in Box 4.2.

Blogs and other social content

Intranet managers often seem unsure whether social media will compete with or complement an intranet, and equally unsure whether such applications should come within the governance structure of the intranet or be governed only by a set of guidelines on what is regarded as good practice in using social media. As with so many internet technologies, applications that started in the consumer market are now moving rapidly into the enterprise market. The range of applications is very wide, and it is not the purpose of this chapter to describe each of them and their use. From an intranet strategy perspective there are some important issues to consider in managing social media channels:

• Where is the interface between the intranet and social media applications?

- Do the social media applications need to meet the quality standards of the intranet content?
- How will social media contributions be found?

Box 4.2 Content publishing personas

Version updater
Scope – Sonia is responsible for ensuring that all the content that she is responsible for is maintained in a current state.

Implication – Sonia needs to be able to replace an existing piece of content with the latest version, revise any relevant hyperlinks and, where needed, transfer the earlier version of the information to a repository.

Project member
Scope – David is a member of a project team and needs to be able to upload a range of content types to the project collaboration application.

Implication – This could be a component of the standard training for projects so that the requirements are placed in context, and the lessons learned from the project could feed back into the training requirements.

Intranet transformer
Scope – Christiane is the intranet co-ordinator for the HR department. As well as adding content she also has responsibility for modifying the navigation so that it reflects the approach that HR is taking in developing the services it offers.

Implication – Changing the information architecture could easily destroy the integrity of the intranet, so this would require some structured training, perhaps by the CMS vendor.

News editor
Scope – Leon is responsible for adding news to the departmental intranet.

Implication – Almost certainly, the news items will involve the use of graphics, and they may need to go through a review workflow. Getting the language right could be a challenge in a multicultural organization. As with any group of personas, it is advisable to start out with perhaps eight or ten and then gradually reduce the number to around four or five. CMSs can be quite frightening applications, and it is essential that content contributors have access to a sand-box area where they can practise their skills without the concern that they might bring down both the intranet and their reputation with a push of the 'Enter' key.

Blogs, in particular, can add a knowledge management dimension to an intranet that can be of great value. They can:

- provide a searchable database of the skills and expertise of staff
- share good practice across the organization
- enable staff to feel engaged with the business
- set and reinforce operational and cultural standards
- support the development of communities
- point to 'best bets' in terms of reports and web resources.

An excellent set of guidance notes has been developed by Richard Dennison and his colleagues at British Telecommunications plc (Box 4.3).[2]

A set of issues for consideration in any internal guidance notes on social media, and blogs in particular, is set out in the Appendix.

Box 4.3 A good blogger

Blogs regularly. Some say three to five times a week is a good number. Others work on a daily routine. Overall, once a week is probably considered the minimum amount.

Should have a distinct voice/personality. You can tell if that person is just copying something or recycling content. While aggregated blogs are okay in some cases, blogs that show that the blogger is a real person help to distinguish one blog from millions of others.

Should be conversational. 'I know I've found a good blogger when I feel like I just had a conversation with that person from reading a post' – much like having a friend or a trusted colleague. Even if the blogger is trying to sell something, he or she shouldn't sound like a salesperson.

Should have good content. Thought-provoking, entertaining, funny, intense, informational, inspirational, deep . . . whatever the style or the subject matter, good content is bound to touch and reach out to the right audience.

Takes the time to respond to comments (or e-mails, messages, etc.). While this may not always be feasible on an individual basis, especially for bigger blogs, it's always good to acknowledge your readers in some way. Individual responses make it personal. But, if that's not possible, a 'mass response' via another blog entry or comment can show your readers that you do pay attention and that you do read and appreciate their comments.

Continued on next page

Box 4.3 (Continued)

Pays attention to spelling and grammar rules. The writing doesn't have to be perfect and typo-free all the time. Even experts and professionals make mistakes. But, if a blogger doesn't try to do a better job at expressing themselves in writing, somehow the message gets lost in the muddle of text that LooKS likE thIS alL tHe tIMe or LIKE THIS.

Learns how to be brave. Blogging can be a very scary business. It's terrifying to put yourself out there. Even if you're not writing about personal stuff, words are very personal things.

Is tenacious/resilient. There are a lot of challenges in the blogosphere: how to learn the technology, how to 'work the web', how to find – and keep – readers, how to get listed in search engines and directories, how to keep up with news, how to come up with content.

Practises blogging ethics/etiquette. Accept mistakes and own up to them, don't copy–paste complete blog entries and articles into your own blogs (that's stealing), among other things.

Knows how to maintain good relationships online. It's more than just responding to comments and e-mails. It's more than just linking, cross-linking, promoting and cross-promoting fellow bloggers. It's about knowing when to assert yourself and when to back down. It's about following up on your word and keeping your promises. It's about respect and responsibility.

Needs a sense of humour!

The social intranet

There is a lot of discussion at present about 'the social intranet', where, in principle, anyone can contribute anything on any topic. Content contribution, as discussed above, is dead; social media applications, on the other hand, will enable all employees to contribute content and comment on the content of others. In principle this is an excellent idea, but there are some issues to take into account that rarely come up in the discussions on this topic:

* It is likely that these social discussions will focus on core business issues, and so significantly elevate the number of items that the search application is going to present to someone looking for the organization's attitude to quality management. Allocating a relevance weighting to social comment is not at all easy, and will need constant monitoring by the search support team.

- There can be some substantial cultural issues, especially in areas of the world where visible disagreement with the views of a manager would be seen as disrespectful.
- Social content is written in a social language, for example English, which might be a challenge for employees not fluent in that language wishing to make comments or take part in the discussion.
- To be pedantic, all content is user-generated unless it originates from outside the organization. There is a sense that 'user-generated content' is not subject to a review process before publication, but in practice the level of review of content published through a CMS is much lower than might have been the case a few years ago.

The use of highly condensed and context-sensitive language is a challenge for information discovery. Navigation, hyperlinks and search all cope poorly with social media, and so, as the volume of social snippets (the description is not in any way derogatory) increases, the challenges of tracking down information will gradually worsen. There is also the issue of archiving, as many of these social contributions will have a lasting value, and archiving may even be a requirement under compliance and audit legislation.

Getting an overall perspective on a topic through integrating social comments and 'formal content', as it is often referred to, is going to take time and effort, and time in particular is in short supply in most organizations.[3,4]

Language management

Most international companies use English as their 'corporate language', and almost certainly the dominant and default language of the intranet will be English. This is not the same as all content being in English, as for national compliance and cultural reasons certain content, especially that relating to employee contracts, will be in one or more of the local languages.

Search applications often highlight the problems of language, even to the extent of having to find out, probably by experiment, whether hit counts on 'colour' and 'color' are the same, to give just one example. The names of many cities are spelled differently in local language and business language. If you have an office in Cologne and want to find out information about the business operations at the office, you will want to get the same number of hits, independent of whether you searched on Cologne, Köln or Koln. And as for transliteration standards for Arabic, have a look at the issues raised by the name of the president of Libya on the *Christian Science Monitor* website.[5]

In some languages the 'alphabetical order' is not intuitive. The scientific term 'angstrom' for sub-molecular distances is named after Anders Jonas Ångstrom, and in Swedish directories Å is listed after Z, not at the end of the A section. There is an extensive suite of ISO standards on transliteration, and intranet managers should be as concerned about using these standards as they are about Web Accessibility Initiative (WAI) standards on accessibility.[6]

One issue that is often overlooked with social media is that not only is a reasonable command of English important, but the user may be using a local-language keyboard to contribute content in English. Try typing the @ symbol on a German-language keyboard, and then try writing a blog entry in English on a Croatian-language keyboard!

Making connections

In any content strategy the need to provide high-quality information about the roles, responsibilities, locations and expertise of employees needs to be high on the agenda. Robertson has written in some detail about the development of staff directories.[7] Social media applications are especially important in enabling people to make connections, the crucial initial step in developing a strong and productive culture of collaboration (see Chapter 5). In the future, when prospective new employees are assessed it may well be that the social networks that a person brings with them will be as important as their education and experience. The new employee will wish to build their own networks as quickly as possible, and indeed may already have identified current employees through Facebook or LinkedIn, resources which may well have provided more information about the company than any corporate presentation is going to do.

In 2007 Deloitte published a very valuable report entitled *Connecting People to What Matters*.[8] The authors note in the introduction:

> In a wired world, connecting people to what matters most is the name of the game. That's because innovation and value emerge primarily out of people's connections. No ideas evolve in isolation; they emerge out of people's interactions. When people are connected, things fall into place. Teams give their best efforts and new products launch on time. The energy is palpable as ideas spring forth and become reality. And when people aren't connected? Strategies fall apart and investors can pull their funds. Executives may get ousted and key people leave – or worse, they stay and complain.

They highlight five reasons for focusing on people's networks and the quality of their relationships, as described in Box 4.4.

Box 4.4 Five reasons to focus on networks and relatonships

Complexity. As jobs become more complex, people are increasingly dependent on one another.
Learning. People learn and create knowledge largely through their interactions with one another.
Decision-making. Leaders make the most effective decisions when they engage stakeholders in respectful ways.
Energy. High-quality interactions create energy. Toxic interactions and conflict avoidance sap energy.
Innovation. Innovators cultivate richer and more diverse networks than their less innovative counterparts.

It is at the point of induction of a new employee, or supporting an employee taking up a new position, perhaps on secondment to a different country, that intranets have always had an important role to play in providing short cuts to corporate policies and procedures. Now, social media can add significantly to the value of the intranet's induction area, and that alone is a major reason for intranet governance to extend to social media governance.

External information

It is very easy to take a blinkered approach to content management, focusing only on internal content, with the result that the intranet creates a corporate information silo in which employees are cut off from external information. The requirement for external information should be driven by the personas and use cases, but because the user groups for external information are often quite small and specialized they can often be overlooked in the content strategy.

Some of the categories that should be considered are:

Business news – There are now many services that will monitor markets and competitors from many thousands of newspapers and periodicals. An important issue with these, and many other external services, is the terms of the licence for use, which may be for a specified group of users, or within a single country. Consideration then has to be given as to how access will be managed for those employees who do have access to the service.

Share price – Where employees have share options, tracking the share price on the relevant stock exchange or exchanges can be a service that is welcomed.

Geo-information – This heading covers weather, maps, satellite imagery and travel conditions.

Extranets

Providing access to the intranet for customers, suppliers and contractors is, in principle, a very effective way of building business relationships, especially when there is a need for collaborative working. However, providing extranet capabilities is fraught with problems, and not just in terms of authentication for access. Content may have to be rewritten for some or all of the external stakeholders, even if it is just to remove internal abbreviations that are meaningless outside the organization. Ensuring that the search application does not retrieve content that should not be available to an external audience can also be a challenge, as the access control lists (ACLs) that are the means of managing secure search are almost invariably based on Active Directory authentication.

It is also very likely that senior managers, especially from the sales department, will wish to be very involved in decisions on what content is made visible, because strategic relationships are at risk. Even for one customer to know that they do not have access and then find that another similar company does could well cause considerable tension both inside and outside the organization.

The development of an extranet should be seen as a separate project, with its own business plan, and it may well require a different steering group that reflects external stakeholder interests. It is not something to be bolted on to an intranet without a significant amount of diligent and considered research and evaluation.

Resources

1 A good introduction to content strategy is given by Anne Rockley in *Managing Enterprise Content*, New Riders, 2003, www.newriders.com.

2 Richard Dennison has written extensively on the use of social media, with particular reference to British Telecom: http://richarddennison.wordpress. com/bts-social-media-guidelines/.

3 There are many books and reports on the subject of social networking and social media. A good starting place is a report from the Nielsen Norman Group based on a synthesis of a number of case studies:Nielsen Norman Group (2009), *Enterprise 2.0: social software on intranets*: www.nngroup.com/ reports/intranet/social/.

4 Laurel Papworth has collected a set of published social media guidelines from a range of organizations: http://laurelpapworth.com/enterprise-list-of-40-social-media-staff-guidelines/.

5 www.csmonitor.com/Commentary/editors-blog/2009/0923/gaddafi-kaddafi-qadhafi-how-do-you-spell-it.

6 Information on the Web Accessibility Initiative (WAI) can be found at: http://www.w3.org/WAI/.

7 Staff directories: www.steptwo.com.au/products/staffdirectories.

8 The report published by Deloitte Consulting is exceptionally well researched and provides guidance on connecting people to organizational culture, resources and colleagues: Deloitte Consulting (2008) *Connecting People to What Matters*, www.deloitte.com/assets/Dcom-UnitedKingdom/ Local%20Assets/Documents/UK_C_ConnectingPeopletoWhatMatters.pdf.

5
Enhancing collaboration

Introduction

Supporting collaborative working has only emerged as an intranet requirement over the last few years, largely as a result of the launch of SharePoint 2007 towards the end of 2006. Of course, there had been collaborative applications before SharePoint 2007 (including SharePoint 2003 and Lotus Notes), but a combination of marketing, functionality and a strong business requirement has brought collaborative applications to the very top of the requirements list of senior managers. This presents a substantial challenge for an intranet manager, because most intranets probably use a CMS application that means they are, essentially, information publishing platforms. WCMSs were not designed to support the often document-intensive world of collaboration, to which social media applications have been bolted on as an afterthought.

The situation is now changing rapidly and an important and far-reaching governance decision is whether the provision and management of collaboration applications should be the responsibility of the intranet manager. This chapter does not set out to be a treatise on collaboration, but only to highlight the issues that should be considered by the intranet team.

The value of collaboration

In 1624 the English metaphysical poet John Donne remarked:

> No man is an island entire of itself; every man
> is a piece of the continent, a part of the main . . .

A more recent poet, John Lennon, wrote in one of the Beatles' songs, 'I get by with a little help from my friends'. In whatever role we play in an organization, the decisions we have to make are challenging ones, and there is a natural urge to share the risk in making a decision, even if it means we may not get all of the due reward.

The critical success factors for collaboration, based on the work by Morten T. Hansen,[1] include:

- a manager with breadth of experience and a reputation across the organization
- a goal that is well defined and measurable
- a goal that people feel passionately about
- a common commitment to finding a solution to the goal
- members of the team who trust each other
- good information from the start
- recognizing that collaboration is a skill
- ensuring that the technology is fit for purpose.

An excellent list of actions that can be taken to achieve excellence in collaboration has been proposed by Logan and Stokes:[2]

- Choose appropriate business projects or accounts as primary collaborative prototypes.

- Develop ways to identify and overcome various barriers to collaboration.
- Establish a comprehensive, continuous learning programme with an emphasis on the skills required for collaboration.
- Establish a communications programme to extol the benefits of collaboration.
- Create organization-wide and local collaboration forums to identify and promote good practice in collaborative working.
- Establish effective intranet-based networks.
- Develop an HR strategy for the recognition and reward of collaborative contributions and results.
- Create the position of chief collaboration co-ordinator.

Many surveys have been undertaken over the last few years which highlight the benefits of collaborative working, but when reading them take care to look at who was asked to take part, the questions they responded to and the company sponsoring the report, before you use the survey data in a business plan.

How well does your organization collaborate?

Rarely is there any evidence from within the organization that the implementation of collaborative technologies will ensure that there is better collaboration, for the simple reason that companies do not assess how well collaboration is taking place. Maishi Nichani, of PebbleRoad, a design consultancy based in Singapore that specializes in intranets and collaboration, has developed a set of seven heuristics that can be used to assess the current state of collaboration in an organization.[3] They are focused on the management side of collaboration rather than on specific collaboration functions. Nichani and his colleagues took this stance because they had seen many ad hoc and headless collaboration efforts that have led to frustration and misery, rather than to sharing and efficiency. The thinking here is that the collaboration effort should be managed with the same rigour and commitment as other business functions, and not be left to chance.

The heuristics are:

- There is a clear business goal for the collaboration set-up.
- There is a clear process for using the collaboration set-up.
- There is a team with necessary skills managing the collaboration set-up.
- There is support and resources available BEFORE using the collaboration set-up.
- There is support and resources available DURING collaboration.
- There is support and resources available AFTER collaboration.
- The collaboration set-up is monitored and evaluated regularly.

Another diagnostic approach is presented by Hansen and focuses on the barriers to collaboration. His view is that these barriers are:

- 'not invented here'
- hoarding
- search problems
- transfer problems.

Hansen has carried out a number of large-scale projects to understand the process of collaboration and how it can be improved. In his book he also presents one of the best-documented examples of how collaboration can have a negative impact on performance.[1] Sterling Software is a highly successful information technology consulting company in the USA. Typically, the sales teams of four to six people would spend two months working on proposals. For some proposals the sales team would bring in other specialists from within the company. Hansen's research showed that the more the teams collaborated, the less chance they had of winning a contract. This seems counter-intuitive. The reason was that the core team had all the experience needed to close the contract. Bringing in other members of staff increased the time and effort expended on a proposal without bringing anything new to the discussions.

The role of the intranet

Some of the above points are issues that an intranet team cannot be expected to solve, but certainly there are many where the intranet can play an important role.

The word 'collaboration' tends to be used as an over-arching term for a range of processes. It can be very helpful to look at elements of these processes in more detail and to identify their roles and where the intranet can make a significant contribution.

The elements are culture, connections, conversations, co-ordination and collaboration. In sequence, they build increasing trust between participants, which is probably the most important success factor for effective collaboration (Figure 5.1). People may enter the sequence at different levels, but will not jump from an initial connection to fully effective collaboration without moving through the intermediate stages.

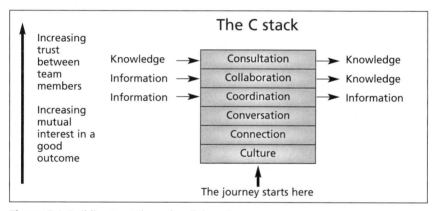

Figure 5.1 Building trust through collaborative processes

Creating a culture

To a very significant extent, employees see senior managers as role models, and this is especially the case with collaboration. Two excellent examples are provided in an article in *Harvard Business Review*.[4]

Case study 5.1 Creating a culture of collaboration

At the Standard Chartered Bank senior executives travel extensively for meetings, and make the effort to publicize these meetings so that the workforce can see that senior managers recognize the importance of face-to-face meetings when important decisions have to be made. Pictures of the management team working with local managers are featured on the intranet. This is just one way in which the executive team sets an example and creates a culture for collaborative working.

At Nokia and BMW, managers have meetings with employees specifically to discuss networking, an approach that is especially important in the case of new employees who want to find and join networks as soon as they can.

The role of the intranet is to ensure that a culture of working together to solve problems is fostered by the organization, and that examples of good practice are highly visible there.

Making connections

Collaboration is all about people working together, so first it is necessary to identify the people who should be brought together. Managers faced with this challenge will rely on their own networks, or more usually the people who report directly to them, as this makes it substantially easier to free up their time to work together. If the objective is to bring together all the relevant experience in the organization, this approach will fail at the first step. Even in a small organization it can be quite difficult to identify who can contribute relevant experience, and in a large multinational organization the challenge is immense.[5-7]

One of the most heavily used applications on most intranets is the staff directory, and yet this is often the subject of a turf war between the intranet team and HR over what information it should include and who is responsible for keeping it up to date. A definitive report on staff directory development has been published by Step Two Designs.[8] What is important from a governance standpoint is that the process for establishing and maintaining the staff directory is agreed, documented and implemented.

Another way in which the knowledge of individual members of staff can be identified is through the use of an enterprise search application, especially where the search application uses entity extraction to highlight names of people not just as authors of documents but because they are listed in the minutes of a meeting or are referred to in an internal report.

Blogs also play a key role in identifying expertise. There can be no doubt that only people who have knowledge and insight, and have the confidence to put this up to peer review across the organization, are going to be effective members of a team. The review process is important, and a good reason why all corporate blogs should have a 'comment' facility.

There is also a place for a 'notice board' to which anyone can post a request for assistance or information. Many organizations seem unduly concerned that it will be misused but, as with so much on an intranet, peer pressure to conform to the way that business is done in the organization is a much better governance mechanism than pages of rules about what can and cannot be posted.

Having conversations

The next step in the process is for the participants selected to work together to begin one-to-one and then one-to-several conversations with other participants, so that information and knowledge can be shared, and even discarded, in the process of developing the scope of the collaboration exercise and defining the current base of information. At this stage a level of trust starts to be built up between all the members of the team so that discussions can be open and constructive. Mutual trust leads to mutual respect.

There is a core role here for the intranet, in integrating social applications such as blogs, instant messages, microblogging, even sticky electronic Post-it notes, all of which can be used to support conversations. Indeed, just having a current telephone directory can be a tremendous asset. How many times has a conversation not taken place simply because you cannot find the current telephone number of the person you wish to speak to? And if the person cannot be found, is there an organization chart from which you can find someone they work with, as another way of starting a conversation?

Co-ordinating resources

Especially with teams that have not worked together before, sharing content with other members of the team is an important prelude to collaboration. A specific task, such as creating a new quality manual, can be split into separate tasks, with individual members of the team submitting drafts of sections but not, at this stage, being involved with the overall development of the manual.

This is where version control on documents becomes very important, and there are two roles here for the intranet team. The first is to make certain that content can be found, through harmonizing the relationship between navigation, hyperlinks and search, each of which plays a role in information discovery. The second is to establish some guidance on how information in a collaboration area relates to information in the intranet. A typical scenario, using Microsoft SharePoint 2007 (MOSS07), is provided in Example 5.1.

···

EXAMPLE 5.1 Collaborating on a new product launch

A project team is given responsibility for developing a launch plan for a new product.

Quite quickly, members of staff find that the content they need for a project, such as document templates, is on the intranet. A copy of the content is made and added to the MOSS07 implementation, almost certainly inside a team site with restricted access permissions.

The project team then finds that it is easier to add additional content to the MOSS07 application through MS Office than by using the intranet CMS. They decide that it would be better to have all the project information on a single application, so other content from the intranet is migrated across, and new content added that might, in the past, have be added to the intranet. The project team also finds that the document template needs to be updated.

Once the project is completed the product launch plan is available to the project team and to anyone to whom the team has e-mailed the launch plan. The updated document template is retained on the MOSS07 application. The project is concluded.

However, the intranet still retains the old document template, but has no copy of the product launch plan, which is still sitting inside the Team Site behind a security firewall. In other words, no one other than the team that worked on it knows that there is a new version.

....

Although the above example uses SharePoint, the problem can arise in any form of team-working application, including a document management application. It is therefore very important that there is very clear governance on the way in which information is added to a collaboration application, and, even more important, on where it is placed after the work has been completed.

Enabling collaboration

Collaboration involves a shared objective and commitment. It has been jointly agreed at the outset that everyone will be affected by the outcome, so both the risks and rewards are shared and there is a high level of trust between all the team members. However, even at this stage problems can arise, especially in the case of multinational and multicultural teams. In the case of multinational intranets, probably the intranet team, and certainly the intranet manager, will be uniquely aware of the challenges faced by teams working in a virtual environment. The collective wisdom on effective team working indicates that getting the participants together in the same location to create effective bonding between team members is an important success factor, but in the current economic climate travel is severely restricted.

Exchanging e-mails and social messages can be much more effective if all parties have some sense of the physical corporate environment, even down to a picture of the desk areas of the participants. The intranet has a role to play here in providing a context for collaboration, and it could include ensuring that information such as current weather conditions and pictures of office or client buildings are available on the intranet. Time-zone information and the means to check local holiday dates are also important, especially when holidays or festivals are based on the lunar calendar. Global meetings calendars can ensure that collaboration sessions are timed for when all the key members of the team are available, an important issue when managing a team whose members may be in multiple locations around the world.

Providing this type of information is really an extension of the content strategy of the intranet. It is included here as an example because few organizations seem to take account of the benefits of such types of information in overcoming the problems of distance and unfamiliarity.

Monitoring impact and performance

It seems that few organizations actively measure the process and impact of collaboration, or make a corporate decision to provide training and support for it. It is always a challenge for an individual to surrender their own personal views, ambitions and prejudices to the greater needs of a team, and the lessons learned need to be highlighted and addressed. In Chapter 13 a range of ways that the value and impact of an intranet can be assessed are set out. These approaches also need to be applied to collaboration assessment, even if the collaboration platform is managed (as is often the case) by the IT department. There is probably no one else in the organization with the remit to do so, other than perhaps a training manager.

This is especially the case in multinational organizations, where the role of a training manager is often at a national level. It can be important to understand where the problems can arise in multinational and multicultural teams (see Box 5.1).

It is easier to design surveys and lessons-learned approaches when problems like these are already recognized. Otherwise a survey may not generate the information needed to enhance the process of collaboration, because staff undertaking it may feel inhibited in highlighting any of these issues, in case they are then seen as not being committed to the organization.

Supporting user adoption

The publication of Michael Sampson's book *User Adoption Strategies*[9] leaves little more to be said about the importance of supporting the use of new technologies – in particular collaboration technologies – by 'Second Wave' staff, who are not by nature early adopters of new technologies.

Box 5.1 The challenges of working in multicltural teams

Jeanne Brett and her colleagues (2006) provide a useful analysis in *Harvard Business Review* of the difficulties people can face when working in multicultural and multinational teams.[7] The following list is based on their work:

- Conflict arises from differences in the way that decisions are made in different countries, or even subsidiaries.
- Misunderstandings arise from the way in which communications are managed. An example would be initially addressing a person by their given name rather than by their family name, in a culture where this is not the norm.
- Violations of hierarchy result in a loss of face.
- Assumptions about the ground rules for a team lead to conflict about schedules and outcomes.
- Team members are inhibited by a perceived difference in status with other members of the team.
- The extent to which a team member is able to take a decision on behalf of colleagues varies across members of the team.

In Chapter 7 of his book Sampson sets out the value of classroom training, web-based training and pages on the intranet for understanding the basic concepts of new collaboration technologies. This is what Sampson has to say about the role of 'Pages on the Intranet' in supporting a user adoption strategy:

Pages on the Intranet

The third strategy for Cultivating Basic Concepts is descriptive Pages on the Intranet.

Description

The Pages on the Intranet strategy involves publishing user-oriented help information to a specified location on the corporate Intranet. When people need to know how to perform a particular task, or use a particular function of the new collaboration technology, they visit the help pages. The help pages contain clear instructions on how to perform the steps involved in the task or function, meaning a user can quickly get on with the task or function without having to interrupt a work colleague.

How to Use It

Write help pages on the tasks or functions people will be doing regularly. The task-focused pages explain how to carry out one of the tasks in a business process – perhaps it's how to set up an idea creation space for an upcoming business planning event, how to start a review of the next press release with input from the external marketing consultancy firm, or how to create a collaboration space for a new team project in the Product Development Group. Task-focused pages demonstrate a function of the collaboration technology within the context of a common business process.

The function-focused pages talk about the basic capabilities of the collaboration technology, but do not discuss how those capabilities can be used in a business process. For example:

- Team projects can be run in a collaboration space. The page on the Intranet would describe what a collaboration space was, and note which tools could be used inside a collaboration space (document sharing, discussion forum, risks and issues register, for example).
- Blogs can be used to share updates with team members and the wider organization. The page would talk about what a blog is, how people get notified, and include links to key internal and external blogs as exemplars.
- Document reviews end when the lead author closes the review cycle and works through the master document to approve or reject proposed changes. The page on the Intranet would talk about how to approve or reject changes.

The two other strategies we have discussed in the chapter derive part of their effectiveness from multimodal learning and social interaction with others. Both of these effectiveness factors can be addressed as part of the strategy:

- Multimodal learning can be offered through embedded videos or recorded demos of particular tasks or functions. Software to record short videos and demonstrations is cheap these days (a few hundred dollars will do it), and will contribute greater learning effectiveness. Pages on the Intranet don't just have to be composed of text! For a great example of multimodal learning, take a look at what Transfield Services in

Australia did when rolling out SharePoint to its employees.

- Social interaction with other people can be offered in a couple of ways. First, the author of the page about a task or function should be listed, so when someone has a question, they know who to contact for further insight. If greater interaction would be beneficial, a discussion forum related to the particular topic could be added.

When to Use It

The Pages on the Intranet strategy has wide applicability for user adoption, but it has a particular role to play when Cultivating Basic Concepts. Classroom training and web seminars will not be able to cover all the required material, and even if they could, people would be unable to retain it. Thus Pages on the Intranet can be used for follow-on descriptive material that will both reinforce the ideas taught through classroom or web seminar methods, as well as extend the learning beyond what either of those modes can do. Trainers in both the classroom and remote situations should make it part of their role to point people to the pages on the Intranet that will help them once they are back in their own work roles.

Why It Works

Pages on the Intranet that explain the basic concepts of the new collaboration technology work for the following reasons:

People can set their own learning pace. Some people will prefer to 'eat everything' in one sitting – they will go through the complete set of pages over a couple of hours so they can see what's there and rapidly learn the basic skills. Others prefer the 'snack and digest' approach, and learn in smaller chunks.

People can focus on what they need to learn. If Christopher already knows the principles in one of the topics, he can skip it and move onto another topic. Christopher isn't inconvenienced by having to wait for a trainer to explain a particular topic to other people, as happens in a classroom environment.

People can learn when they need to. The pages on the Intranet are available at any time for Christopher to review. He isn't limited to learning new material when resident expert Sally is in the office.

Directing people to pages on the Intranet can be a useful part of an overall user adoption approach, but don't make it the totality of your approach. It will always be the case that targeted training material that speaks to a particular context and work role will be more valuable than generic training material that talks about the capabilities of a tool. That's just the way it is – not just with Central Desktop, but with other tools too. The trick is to use the best of both approaches – the training materials available from the vendor for training on basic concepts, and the specific training material showing how a particular team, group or organization is going to make use of the tool's capabilities for their own work.

Resources

1   Morten Hansen provides a wealth of information and inspiration on the subject of collaboration, based on many years of large-scale research projects:
    Hansen, M. T. (2009) *Collaboration*, Boston, MA: Harvard Business School Press, www.thecollaborationbook.com/.

2   Logan, R. K. and Stokes, L. W. (2004) *Collaborate To Compete*, New York: Wiley.

3   www.pebbleroad.com/articles/view/reviewing-intranet-based-collaboration-setups.

4   Gratton, L. and Ericsson, T. J. (2007) Ways to Build Collaborative Teams, *Harvard Business Review*, November, 101–9.

5   Why Teams Don't Work – An interview with Diane Coutu, *Harvard Business Review*, May 2009, 99–105.

6   McDermott, R. and Archibald, D. (2010) Harnessing your Staff's Informal Networks, *Harvard Business Review*, March, 83–9.

7   Brett, J., Behfar, K. and Kern, M. C. (2006) Managing Multicultural Teams, *Harvard Business Review*, November, 84-91.

8   James Robertson and Donna Maurer have written a very practical handbook on building and maintaining staff directories:
    www.steptwo.com.au/products/staffdirectories.

9   Michael Sampson (www.michaelsampson.net) is a consultant who specializes in collaboration, and has written a number of excellent books on the subject, many with a strong SharePoint element:

Sampson, M. (2009) *Seamless Teamwork*, Redmond, WA: Microsoft Press.

Sampson, M. (2009) *SharePoint Roadmap for Collaboration*, Christchurch, New Zealand: The Michael Sampson Company.

Sampson, M. (2010) *User Adoption Strategies*, Christchurch, New Zealand: The Michael Sampson Company.

Part 2
Technology

6

Managing technology

Introduction

Intranet managers are often in the position of having to use whatever technology is available, and often this is a WCMS application, and even a search application, that is being used for the organization's website. Microsoft Office SharePoint Server 2007 (often abbreviated to MOSS07) has been implemented by organizations as a generic information management and collaboration platform, and is often offered to the intranet manager as the solution to all their problems. Microsoft SharePoint 2010 is now available and organizations are in the process of deciding whether or not to upgrade, and when to do so.

Provided that the WMCS and search applications meet the requirements of the intranet then it makes good business sense to gain the most from the investment. If this is not the case then the future development of the intranet can be seriously affected. Another technology issue that faces intranet managers is that increasingly the intranet is a gateway into other applications, and this can give rise to not only technology issues (which can usually be solved) but also information authentication and security management issues, which can be much more difficult to solve.

Even if the intranet manager is not in total command of the technology platforms available the intranet needs to have a technology strategy so that the implications of changes in the applications available can be clearly determined, and the risks and benefits assessed.

Web content management

Although there is some commonality between presenting content on a website and on an intranet, there are also some significant differences. That does not mean that a CMS designed for website use, with sophisticated graphics management and built-in e-marketing and e-commerce applications, will not be suitable for an intranet, but it is unlikely that this will be the case. The main differences between an intranet and a website are described in the following sections.

Distributed content contribution

Websites are usually maintained by a core staff of specialists, either within the organization or at an agency, who take content from departments of the organization and add it to the website. They become power users, very familiar with short cuts through the application, and often have a significant amount of technical expertise in HTML and XML.

Intranet content should be able to be contributed by anyone in the organization. However, this is not the same as 'everyone'! Content contributors may only be adding an event every couple of months, or a marketing report at the end of each month, and they will expect the process of adding content to be about as easy as attaching a document to an e-mail. If it is not, then they will attach a document to an e-mail as a way of publishing information to the organization. This means that the CMS has to support a range of content contribution routes, from a simple e-form right up to a major reorganization of the information architecture of the site to cope with acquiring a new business. Training needs to be modular, to cater for all levels of need, and excellent online contextual help options should be available. The content contributor may need to train their successor without any help from the intranet team, who may be thousands of miles away.

Authentication

Websites are usually locked down to the website team, and all the content is publicly on show, albeit with some password-protected areas. In an intranet the situation is totally different. There has to be scope for granular permissioning of content contributors, so that some contributors can only edit existing pages and others can create microsites or new sections of the intranet. There will also be controls on access to certain content (for example, management reports) so that confidential information remains confidential. This is usually managed by linking every content contributor and every user to an access permissions database built around the Active Directory (AD) used for employee authentication into corporate systems. Access by external stakeholders to an extranet will be managed by passwords, adding to the complexity of managing access. The CMS will need to be able to use the corporate AD database, and that can be a considerable technical and political challenge because the groups set up on the AD may not match the circulation lists for intranet content.

The authentication issue becomes even more complicated when a search function is added. It will then be necessary to ensure that only people with permission to see the content can see the summary information in the search results. These permissions are handled by access control lists (ACLs), which usually match the AD groups, but not always.

The above is a very brief summary of authentication issues, but shows why it is very important to be able to manage contribution and access permissions with ease from within the CMS (and search) administration areas.

Document management

Many intranets are, in effect, document management systems with a web front end. Especially in industries with a need to meet compliance requirements, version control of documents is of crucial importance. Often companies in these industries will have tightly controlled document management and records management applications, which need to be integrated into the intranet and the search application. In a website the number of word-processing and PDF documents is usually quite low and these documents will not be subject to constant revision in the way that is typical for internal documents. As a result, many CMS products aimed at the website market have only limited document management capabilities. These may be sufficient for smaller organizations, but particular care needs to be taken to ensure that document management requirements are clearly defined.

Integration with other applications

Websites tend to be stand-alone applications that are often externally hosted. They may need to link in to other systems for e-commerce applications, but in general all related applications will be co-hosted. In the case of an intranet there may be a requirement to link in to an HR system for a staff directory, a finance system for expenses claims, an enterprise resource planning system for product information and an external database provider (such as Lexis-Nexis) for information research and news services. All these services need to manage access authentication from the intranet platform, and additional information may need to be provided through the authentication so that, if necessary, changes can be made to the other systems. An example would be to enable a member of staff to revise their entry in the staff database managed by HR. This is another area where some website CMS products might well fail to provide the relevant functionality, or where to do so might require extensive and expensive customization.

Running the intranet and the website on separate platforms will also reduce the risk in having all the web assets of the organization on an application from a single vendor. Also, there could be an important technical or business case for changing either the intranet or the website WCMS (for example, so as to have better shopping-cart features on the website), and if there were only a single platform all the upgrade and migration work for both applications would have to be undertaken simultaneously.

IT departments often do not want to be in the position of supporting two different platforms. In principle, this is quite understandable, but in practice the level of support needed for a CMS will generally be very low, unless a high level of internal development is undertaken. This situation usually only arises when Microsoft SharePoint is the core application. In such situations the best way to reassure the IT department is to have some reference cases from the vendors that illustrate the low level of support.

Personalization and customization

For over a decade there has been continuing interest in the ability to provide personalized and customized content to users, perhaps through the use of portal technology. The usual catalyst for this is complaints about not being able to find information, and comments that it would be so good to be able to open the intranet in the morning and see just information that the user needs for the day ahead.

There is some debate as to the difference between personalization and customization. Generally speaking, customization relates to presenting content that is role-based, so that a marketing manager does not see content that is specific to a research and development manager, for example. Roles may also be based on a management hierarchy, with a senior management portal, for example, providing access to business intelligence applications that are not generally accessible to all employees.

Personalization takes the concept one stage further, with an individual member of staff being able to choose either all, or a selection, of content that they find they need on a day-to-day basis. In principle, this is a good idea, but in practice a number of issues arise, including:

1 A concern that users may decide not to see the news pages, so the
   concept of the intranet as a means of setting organizational
   agendas through news and comment is challenged.
2 The time available to users to develop and modify their profiles so
   that the content continues to match their requirements.
3 How to alert users to the availability of all the content they might
   be interested in but are not currently aware of.
4 The limits on screen real-estate, which even with sophisticated
   portal software limits the number of portlets to perhaps 10 at the
   most, when there may well be 50 or more available.
5 The unpredictability of the working day, with the result that users
   become frustrated at having to override their custom setting.

No matter what WCMS and portal vendors may say, managing
personalization and customization is a complex and time-consuming
process, and before upgrading an intranet to offer a level of either
customization or personalization, it is essential to visit other
organizations that have used the same WCMS or portal application and
talk about the support-staff time involved.

Intranet and enterprise search

Organizations have only recently begun to realize the importance of
effective search on an intranet.

Some organizations have made do with the search functionality of the
WCMS, but this only indexes the content on the WCMS server.
However, most organizations fail to realize that getting the best from the
search investment requires a dedicated support team with IT, business
and taxonomy skills, which could easily be a team of four people. The
search logs are an invaluable source of information not only about what
users can find but also about what they are looking for and cannot find.
In the latter case there may need to be changes to the information
architecture or to the metadata schema, and these are not changes that
can be made in a matter of hours, or even days. Such is the level of

performance that users have come to expect from Google on the world wide web that any apparent failure of the search application to find information that is known to exist will quickly result in a permanent loss of trust in the search application.

The annual survey *Global Intranet Trends* has indicated for a number of years that search is regarded as a core application and yet the level of satisfaction is very low. In the 2010 survey only 14% of respondents were very satisfied with their search application. Certainly, 47% were moderately satisfied, but this is not an acceptable benchmark for search.

Why are the results so poor? Only 12% of respondents to the survey had a search strategy for implementation and evolution and in only 6% of cases were business owners involved in defining requirements. Users were consulted about search requirements by only 10% of the respondents and just 13% conducted usability tests. Those figures are bad enough, but there are worse. In 70% of organizations there was less than one full-time employee working on search support; 30% of organizations did not look at search logs at all, and a further 35% did so only when resources allow.

What seems to be happening is that the blame for poor search results is being pinned on the technology, as a third of all respondents had implemented a new search application in the past 12 months or were in the process of implementing one. This is good news for the search vendors, but not for employees in the organizations concerned.

Although search will be an element of the personas, it can be useful to take a complementary approach to understanding the use cases for search. Four use cases are set out in Table 6.1, using a corporate compliance manager as an example.

Intranet search quickly becomes an issue of providing enterprise search, in which multiple repositories and applications are searched on a federated basis. This brings with it a multiplicity of issues surrounding the presentation of results in a helpful sequence from these repositories, and substantial issues over security management. As mobile access to the intranet increases, there is also a need to factor in providing a search solution that takes advantage of the positional information that can be derived from the mobile device to customize a location-specific results set.

In considering what the strategy for providing search should be, it is important to take a wider view of information discovery. The four ways in which a user discovers information are through:

- lists and structured navigation
- hyperlinks
- search
- alerts.

All too often the solution to complaints about inability to find inform-ation is to provide a search engine. However, search is not the ubiquitous discovery solution. For example, a hyperlink is a contrib-ution of knowledge to a web page. Hyperlinks are generally added manually; the person who adds the link is using their expertise to relate to documents, and that expertise can be of immense value to others, especially in the learning/exploratory use case described in Table 6.1.

Table 6.1 Use cases for intranet search functionality				
	Known item	**Learning/ exploratory**	**Parametric**	**Thematic**
Use case	The user wants to find a single and specific item and knows how and where to look for it.	The user wants to find information that will help them to learn something, and therefore may have a poorly defined query.	The user knows the criteria for the result set, even though they may not know the specific items that will be found.	The user is familiar with the subject area and is able to frame the query, based on expertise.
Compliance manager	I need the latest issue of the corporate compliance guidelines.	I need to know more about how our commitment to a carbon-free environment might impact my review of our procedures.	I need to find the reference to a comment about how our competitors treat compliance risks that was brought up at the May meeting of the Archimedes Project team.	I need to be able to compare the EU and US standards on waste water treatment.

External hosting of an intranet CMS

An intranet is hosted internally on the organization's servers. For larger organizations, especially where there is a requirement to interface with other enterprise applications, this is probably essential so as to maintain security and system performance. However, external hosting should not be dismissed without due deliberation on the benefits and challenges. As a precursor to implementing cloud computing, a number of companies are now developing a Software as a Service (SaaS) option. Another driver for hosted solution could be the move towards social intranets, where links to applications such as Facebook and LinkedIn will be increasingly important. External hosting may also provide better location-independent support.

Hybrid solutions are also possible. Although these will require careful synchronization between the hosted and internal applications, the benefits could be considerable. The choice of SaaS CMS products is still quite limited, but this will change significantly as companies begin to look at ways of providing cloud computing.

An issue that does need to be carefully considered with SaaS applications is the way in which enterprise search will be provided if the search application extends beyond the intranet, to index and search document management and other internal repositories.

Cloud computing

A technology that could have major implications for intranet managers is cloud computing. In principle, this technology is similar to the bureau computer services that became available in the 1980s, with the difference that cloud services are much more scalable and flexible, using the internet as the backbone network. It probably represents a technology shift as significant as the internet itself.

For many organizations, especially in the face of constraints in IT investment, the economic advantages of not having to invest in any hardware for the IT suite, and of being able to use a wide range of software applications through SaaS offerings from the cloud service vendors, will be considerable. It is interesting to note that Microsoft has made significant changes to SharePoint 2010 so as to be ready to take advantage of cloud computing.

The challenge for intranet managers, especially those in larger organizations, is to understand the implications and benefits of cloud computing if they are not to face a situation similar to that which many have experienced with SharePoint, in which the IT department fails to appreciate some of the subtleties of how the intranet platform is managed.

Certainly one of the implications will be how to manage data privacy when the organization has no say in where data that is subject to privacy legislation will reside. Although there is at present a lot of discussion on this subject, and Hewlett Packard (HP) in particular has looked into the legal issues that need to be addressed, legislative changes to accommodate cloud computing will take some time to come on to the statute book, and in the meantime only contract law will be available as a way of managing how data privacy is maintained.

Social media and collaboration applications

Content management, document management and search have historically been the three core platforms for an intranet, but this is changing rapidly as applications to support collaboration and social media begin to be widely implemented to meet user and business requirements. IT departments may well be familiar with the collaboration and social media applications embedded into Microsoft SharePoint and IBM WebSphere, but may have little knowledge of the dozens of individual applications and application suites that are also available.

As with anything else intranet-related, it is vital to understand user requirements, and in the case of collaboration and social media some element of forecasting future requirements is very important, taking into account the demographic profile of the organization.

Another issue that social media bring to the table is the extent to which the organization bars access to sites such as Facebook, LinkedIn and YouTube. Organizations may be justifying limitation of access by anecdotal stories about security breaches and inappropriate use. The number of subscribers to applications such as Facebook (500 million at the time of writing) means that any future social media strategy that is based on barring access and providing some form of internal social networking option will not be sustainable for more than a year or two at most. The benefits to the organization of having employees connect to a global network will far outweigh concerns about time being wasted by staff or networks being overloaded by YouTube videos.

This is a sensitive issue, and is probably best resolved by all the stakeholders setting down their views on paper for careful consideration, rather than by having a meeting where seniority outweighs democracy and leading to decisions being made by managers who may have very little regular experience of the value of these social media applications.

Mobile access to intranets

Once upon a time, when the pilot shut down the engines of the aircraft, there was a short period of calm as passengers readied themselves for the torment of the baggage carousel. Now the silence is broken by the noise of mobile phones being switched on and the beeps of messages arriving. We live in a world where being away from e-mail and text messages for even an hour means that we are concerned that decisions have been made without our invaluable input.

Over the last couple of years the mobile handset has changed beyond all recognition. The Apple iPhone and the Google Android are changing the mobile paradigm from messaging to information and application access. However, possibly the most important recent development has had much less visibility, and that is the purchase of Palm by HP. HP's interest is not in Palm hardware but in the WebOS operating system and a raft of 1500 patents on mobile information access that Palm has not had the resources to develop any further.

To return to the aircraft for a moment, one of the outcomes of the disruption of European air traffic caused by the Icelandic volcano in 2010 was that staff at all levels found themselves working from hotel rooms and airports – often without a laptop, as they were returning from holidays. Their Smartphone could act as an effective e-mail access device, but most were marooned from their corporate intranet. In this situation, just tracking down staff telephone numbers on the corporate directory became a nightmare.

Without any doubt, the mobile handset business, driven by consumer demand, will have a transforming influence on intranets. Organizations will need to have a mobile access strategy for their intranet if they do not want their employees to be at a major competitive disadvantage. It is not necessary to provide access to all intranet content, but simply to focus on delivering content that is of particular value to staff who find themselves rewarded for being out of the building, and then penalized by not having access to the intranet. Indeed, a good way to start is to add a new persona to your collection that summarizes the key requirements of mobile staff. This is not just a senior executive issue, but ripples all the way down to people just starting out on their careers and for whom the mobile handset is the way they live and wish to work.

One technology issue that needs careful consideration is mobile search, though GPS information can be used very effectively to limit search queries and results to those relevant to the user's precise location. Rarely will a project manager in Germany be interested in projects being carried out in Brunei!

So far the level of adoption of mobile access has been quite low, but this is probably because organizations are waiting to see who the winner will be in the corporate mobile applications market, with Apple, Google (Android), RIM (BlackBerry), Nokia and Microsoft all having a keen interest in developing this market.

Bandwidth management

Discussions about intranet IT platforms often focus on hardware and software issues, and on network security. What is often overlooked is the available bandwidth for intranet access, especially in locations in countries that have limited terrestrial network bandwidth for internet access. The wide use of mobile telephony in Africa and India is largely because mobile access is easier to install than high-bandwidth cable or fibre-optic networks. Search applications, in particular, can be a problem for users viewing large numbers of individual documents when hunting for information. There are many solutions to bandwidth management, including local search, low-graphics options on intranet pages, good document summaries to help evaluation of relevance, and local caching of core documents.

Enterprise architecture

In the late 1980s it was becoming obvious that organizations were spending more and more money building IT systems, and at the same time finding it increasingly difficult to keep increasingly expensive IT systems aligned with business needs. The seminal paper that marked the start of considering IT systems and processes within an overall architecture was 'A Framework for Information Systems Architecture' (Zachman, 1987). There are now four widely used enterprise architecture models:

- the Zachman Framework for Enterprise Architectures
- The Open Group Architectural Framework (TOGAF)
- the Federal Enterprise Architecture
- the Gartner Methodology.

As intranets and related applications (enterprise search in particular) continue to increase in the value they bring to the organization, the more important it will be for all stakeholders to see the intranet positioned within the agreed enterprise architecture.[1,2,3] For the same reason the content of the intranet also needs to be positioned within an information management architecture (see Chapter 18); so far, relatively little work has been carried out, other than by Gartner, to bring together best practice in enterprise architecture and information management into an information governance architecture.

Frustrating though it can be for the intranet team, the requirements of the existing enterprise architecture have to be taken into account when considering the IT strategy for the intranet. The simple fact that an intranet is different is not a business case for ignoring the enterprise architecture and related information systems strategy.

Resources

1   Roger Sessions gives a summary of the different approaches to enterprise architecture:
    http://msdn.microsoft.com/en-us/library/bb466232.aspx.

2   A very readable account of Zachmann's work (1987) can be found in the
    Wikipedia entry at
    http://en.wikipedia.org/wiki/Zachman_Framework, which provides
    numerous references.
3   Zachman, J. A. (1987), A Framework for Information Systems
    Architecture, *IBM Systems Journal*, **26** (3), 276-92.

The following resources cover a wide range of intranet related
technologies:

*   The technology blogs on ZD Net are a good way to track developments in
    a wide range of enterprise technologies:
    www.zdnet.com.
*   The portal of the Association for Computing Machinery contains a wealth
    of papers on all aspects of intranet-related technologies, but this is only
    accessible by members of the ACM:
    www.acm.org.
*   Stephen Arnold and I have written a book on enterprise search
    management:
    Arnold, S. and White, M. (2010) *Successful Enterprise Search Management*,
    Manchester: Galatea Publishing, www.galatea.co.uk.
*   The technical reports from the research laboratories of Hewlett Packard
    are a useful source of information on emerging technologies, especially on
    cloud computing and also enterprise search:
    www.hpl.hp.com/techreports/.
*   Stephen Arnold monitors developments in search technology :
    http://arnoldit.com/wordpress/.
*   The Real Story Group (www.realstorygroup.com) publishes vendor-
    neutral comparative reviews of products in the following categories:
    — collaboration and community software
    — component content management
    — digital asset management
    — e-mail archiving and management
    — enterprise content management
    — evaluating SharePoint
    — portals and content integration

- — search and information access
- — SharePoint across the enterprise
- — web analytics
- — web content management.
- CMSWire tracks developments in CMS, ECM and search tecnologies: www.cmswire.com.

7
Specifying and selecting software

Introduction

Intranet managers often find that they are directly involved in decisions about selecting a new CMS or search application. Usually this is driven by the apparent inability of the current CMS to meet requirements; sometimes by concern about the level of technical support from the vendor, systems integrator or internal resources. In larger companies it is not unusual for there to be more than one CMS in use, especially if the company has grown through acquisition, and often there can be different version releases of the same CMS. Another common scenario is that the intranet and the website both use the same CMS; there is a good business case for changing the CMS to meet the website requirements, resulting in the intranet ending up on a totally unsuitable platform.

Specifying and selecting new CMS, search, social media and collaboration software can be quite challenging, because the daily management of the intranet has to be continued, and on top of this work a substantial amount of time will have to be dedicated to the process of selecting and implementing the software. The process will involve working very closely with an IT department, which is unlikely to be able to offer much experience of CMS and search software to the intranet team.

Over the last few years the selection process has moved on from being one in which vendors were provided with a table of functional requirements and the responses were scored and tabulated so that the vendor with the highest score could be given the contract. (And it was not unusual for there to be several hundred requirements.) The focus has now switched to being one in which the emphasis is not on what might be regarded as the nominal functionality of the application, but on what the application will enable the organization to achieve.[1]

Intranet content management

The main differences between an intranet and a website, which may make a CMS designed for website use unsuitable for an intranet, have been summarized in Chapter 6.

There are many different CMS solutions for intranets, ranging in price from zero- or nominal-cost open-source applications right up to portal products such as IBM WebSphere. Somewhere in the middle in cost terms comes Microsoft SharePoint. Especially in the UK, there are an increasing number of intranet-specific applications that have modules for everything from expenses-form management to meeting-room booking. With the exception of the intranet-specific applications, the research products from the Real Story Group (formerly CMS Watch)[2] remain the definitive source of information on the comparative strengths and weaknesses of not only CMS products but also search and collaboration applications.

Before undertaking the user requirements research and reviewing the vendor options for either CMS or search applications, some fundamental issues need to be considered:

- Will the organization be dealing with the vendor directly or through an integration partner? Maintaining project momentum and communication is significantly more difficult when there is an integration partner, especially if it is not familiar with the latest version of the application.
- If there is an incumbent integration partner or IT systems have been outsourced, will this limit the range of options that can be considered, as these organizations tend to work only with a few vendors?
- If the organization is located in a number of different countries will the vendor/integrator be able to provide an acceptable level of local support?
- When the procurement budget was set was the cost of implementation taken into account? This can vary by a factor of from one to four times the base licence cost on top of the licence costs themselves. A CMS with a licence cost of £100,000 might well cost upwards of £250,000 to implement.
- In view of the fact that the procurement process may take a year from start to installation, has the fact that costs may end up being incurred in the next financial year been taken into account?
- What other projects are planned for the period of procurement and implementation that might have an impact on the requirements for the intranet or on the IT resources available for implementation? A move to a cloud computing environment might give rise to some difficult data privacy issues for an intranet application.
- Again, given the length of time it will take to select and implement the product, is there a product development roadmap that might indicate an opportune moment to start the project? Installing Version 6.7 and then finding three months later that Version 7.0 would meet user requirements without any need for the customization involved in implementing Version 6.7 should be avoided at all costs.

Project planning for software implementation

The basic structure of the project plan is the same for CMS and for search applications, and indeed for any software selection project. Table 7.1 provides some indicative timings to illustrate the total time required from the start of the project, through implementation to a successful launch.

Migration management

The primary reason for a WCMS project not meeting the expected schedule is that it is very difficult to anticipate the work that will be involved in migrating content to a new application, especially if the content architecture is to be changed at the same time. WCMS vendors tend to downplay the complexity of the task, as they do not want to raise concerns about whether or not they are the best choice of vendor. From a customer perspective, there is probably no recent experience of migration within the organization from which to gain a first-hand view of the issues.

What is often overlooked is that most of the intranet content contributors will have to be engaged in the migration process, and yet the benefit to them of undertaking the work is minimal. Certainly content contribution may be easier for them in future, but that is not going to offset the many days of patient work under severe time pressure to meet the promised launch date of the new WCMS.

The strategic reason for raising the issue of migration is to ensure that when the schedule is drawn up for a new WCMS, or even a major upgrade to the current WCMS, the time needed for content migration will be included in the project plan. Even a major upgrade may cause problems if the current version has been highly customized, meaning that while the upgraded version may offer better functionality in certain areas, a period of development work will be necessary before the content can be added.

Table 7.1 Project timings, from start to launch		
Project stage	**Scope and comments**	**Time to complete**
User requirements	Determination of the requirements of both end users and content contributors.	1 month
Preparation of RFP (invitation to tender)	Some organizations initially prepare a request for information, which will add another month or so to the project schedule without saving a similar amount of time later in the project.	1 month
Vendor proposal submission	It will take a vendor at least three weeks to prepare a proposal. In the public sector some procurement requirements may extend the time that has to be given to vendors.	1 month
Proposal review	Reading through the proposals and coming to a consensus on a short list of vendors to invite to give a presentation always takes much longer than anticipated.	1 month
Vendor invitations	Since many CMS and search vendors are quite small businesses they will need some time to prepare for a presentation. Even if the dates for the demonstrations are given in the RFP, most vendors will need at least 2–3 weeks to prepare for the meeting.	1 month
Selection of a vendor	After the meetings a preferred vendor will be identified. The vendor will then wish to conduct further research before presenting a quotation and project plan.	1 month
Contract agreement and installation	It may well take a further month to agree all the contractual details, and another month before the vendor can get on site and install the software.	2 months
Implementation	During this stage all the customization takes place, the initial uploading of content occurs, and training begins.	2–3 months for a small intranet, but perhaps 6 months for a portal application
Migration	See later in table.	3 months
Launch		13–17 months in total

Writing the request for proposal

Table 7.2 sets out the main sections of any request for proposal (RFP).[3]

Table 7.2 Request for proposal – main sections

Section	Content
Evaluation process	Sets out the schedule for the evaluation process so that this is clear from the outset. Include the dates for the evaluation demonstrations. Also include the overall project schedule and the total budget available.
Business overview	Brief account of the company and the role played by the intranets.
Project team	The structure of the project team and the people who will be involved in the selection and implementation process. Include details of internal development resource.
Current intranet	Description of the current platforms, number of users and content contributors, size of the intranets, any applications or customized features developed specifically for the intranet, and why these are important, where the CMS works well, and any problems.
Reasons for the change	Statement of what the organization is aiming to achieve through the procurement of new software.
IT overview	IT architecture, hosting requirements, security and authentication, search application and any constraints that might influence the selection of a CMS or search application. Also in this section, state who will be involved in developing templates/style sheets, etc.
Objectives for the new CMS	States the key priorities for the application, so that they will also shape the priorities for functionality.
Use cases	States in scenario form the way in which the intranet will be used, and what are regarded by different sets of stakeholders as critical success factors, such as ease of content addition. There may be more scenarios in this section than will be evaluated at the demonstration meetings.
Information architecture	Sets out any changes that are proposed in the structure of the site.
Specific functional requirements	Lists any functional requirements that are project-critical, relating them back to the scenarios to show why they are important. Security management may be especially important.
Roadmap	The roadmap for the software over the next year; what will be released between signing the contract and implementation of the software, and the impact this will have on the project, especially if it falls behind the release schedule.
Reference customers	Details of reference customers using the current version of the software, and that similar in scale and scope to organization.
Project milestones	Identification by the vendor of project milestones, and of factors that might advance or delay them.
	Continued on next page

Table 7.2 (Continued)	
Section	Content
Training	Training that the vendor will provide for content contributors and systems administration staff.
Migration	How the vendor proposes to approach the issue of migration of content from the current systems.
Vendor requirements	What the vendor needs from the organization so as to ensure success of the project, e.g. access to a development server by a particular date.
Risks	What the vendor see as the risks for project completion on time and within budget, and how they will be addressed.
Financial proposal	Sets out the fixed and variable costs, and the cost of the implementation.
Terms and conditions	Standard terms and conditions for software procurement.

Probably the most important element of the RFP will be some use cases for the way in which the CMS will be used to support content contribution to the intranet. In Example 7.1 brief profiles of the people concerned are provided in the preamble.

EXAMPLE 7.1 Use case – CMS content contributors

1 Ian has prepared a new version of the corporate Quality Manual, which is a 40-page Word document. Amanda is the content manager for the Quality Department, and she needs to be able to convert the Word document into sections that can be presented as HTML pages within sections. Each section should have anchor text, and the set of subheadings needs to be positioned at the beginning of the document.

2 Amanda also needs to create a synopsis of the document to act as an HTML header for both the HTML version, which is not a controlled document, and the locked-down PDF version of the document, which is the definitive version.

3 The synopsis needs to be reviewed and approved by Ian before publication.

4 The Quality Manual refers to other corporate documents, and Amanda needs to identify links to other documents and URLs elsewhere on the intranet. She also needs to be able to identify links that others have made to the Quality Manual, and alert the authors of these links that the

Quality Manual has been revised.

5 One of the sections of the Manual needs to link to an internal video showing how to perform the final check on the equipment before despatch to a customer. Amanda needs to link to this video, and also to provide a link to a PowerPoint file of pictures that illustrate the process for the factory in Thailand, which does not always have good internet access.

6 Because the document is one that all production managers need to have read and accepted, Amanda needs a means of ensuring that all the relevant managers have read the document and completed a short online test to check that they have understood the main changes in this version.

7 Amanda will set a date for the next review of the document. When she publishes the new version she will move the previous version to an archive repository.

••

Here the Quality Manual is used as an example of any corporate document for which the organization has a compliance requirement, in this case under ISO 9000.

Using this approach makes it easy for the CMS vendor to illustrate both in the tender document and in any later evaluation meeting how the functionality of the product will meet these requirements. From the organization's viewpoint it will also be clear that this core business process can be met by the vendor, and in effect form the basis of the contract in due course.

There is just one example of use case, and there may well be eight or ten in all. Beyond this point, the law of diminishing returns tends to come into play.

Search application selection

In the case of search, the unknown factor is not migration, but the way in which the relevance of content is managed once the initial crawl has taken place.[4] The similarity to content migration for a new CMS is that any problems, not only of relevance but also of management of security permissions, will only become apparent once the application has been installed and initially configured. The problems are unlikely to be on the same scale as for content migration, but some float should be built into the project schedule to resolve them.

Resources

1 I have written about the specification and selection of content management and search software in two books published by Facet Publishing (www.facetpublishing.co.uk):
    White, M. (2005) *The Content Management Handbook*, London: Facet Publishing.
    White, M. (2007) *Making Search Work: implementing web, intranet and enterprise search*, London: Facet Publishing.
2 Real Story Group: www.realstorygroup.com.
3 Step Two Designs publishes the *Content Management Toolkit*, which is a comprehensive list of CMS features and a methodology for the procurement process:
    www.steptwo.com.au/products/toolkit.
4 Stephen Arnold and I went into more detail on the subject in: Arnold, S. and White, M. (2009) *Successful Enterprise Search Management*, Manchester: Galatea Publishing, www.galatea.co.uk.

8

Using Microsoft SharePoint for intranets

Introduction

The global adoption of Microsoft SharePoint by organizations of all sizes means that in a book that is in other respects resolutely vendor neutral it is important to highlight the benefits and issues that arise when considering the use of SharePoint for an intranet. The core problem is that often there is no opportunity to consider the use of SharePoint because the decision has already been made by the IT department to implement it. The intranet manager is then faced with the decision of how best to make use of the situation.

This chapter does not attempt to provide a technical evaluation of either Microsoft SharePoint 2007 (often abbreviated to MOSS07) or Microsoft SharePoint 2010 (SP2010). A report from the Intranet Benchmarking Forum looks in detail at how SP2010 can be used for an intranet; there is also a report from the Forum on MOSS07.[1] The Real Story Group offers a set of detailed evaluations of SharePoint and these are essential reading for any intranet manager who is unfamiliar with the product suite.

As the notional owners of the SharePoint application will be the IT department, and because SharePoint is a development platform, IT will almost certainly wish to take a lead in setting the implementation objectives and timetable. SharePoint is certainly a development platform, but it is equally a business delivery platform. The business has to set and assess the progress towards meeting clear business objectives. This is especially challenging with SharePoint because some departments may want to use just one functional area while others may require several areas to be developed in parallel and integrated together.

There is no doubt that good intranets can be built using MOSS07 or SP2010, and indeed some of the intranets described in the Nielsen Norman *Annual Intranet Design* reports[2] do use MOSS07 as their platform. However, there are probably a much greater number of intranets where the move to a SharePoint application has not met expectations.[3] This is almost always the result of:

- a failure to put into place a governance strategy at the outset of the implementation
- a failure to recognize that there will be a need to undertake a lot of customization of SharePoint, especially if the current features of an intranet on a WCMS are to be matched
- a failure to realize that, certainly in the case of MOSS07, none of the individual elements of the application is even close to best of breed (SP2010 is significantly better in this respect)
- a failure to realize that SharePoint is not 'free': someone has had to pay for the licences and there will be some significant development costs.

A particular challenge for intranet managers is that, even if there is no pressure to move the intranet to SharePoint for content management purposes, there is likely to be extensive use of the application for collaborative working. This will almost certainly give rise to scenarios along the following lines:

- A project team is set up to prepare a report on new business opportunities in the Middle East.

- The team sets up a team site in SharePoint, locates work previously carried out on this market from the intranet, and adds copies of it to the team site.
- Membership of the team site is restricted to the project team of ten people. Because of the way in which secure search is implemented, none of the work in progress, and maybe not even the existence of the project team, will be identified in a search.
- Once the project has finished the final report may be sent to a group of senior managers, and no further use will be made of that particular team site.

The end result will be that the report will disappear, unless a procedure is in place to ensure that the document is published on the intranet or the team site is opened up to all members of staff.

Both the technology strategy and the content strategy for an intranet where there is also a SharePoint implementation have to focus on the grey area between two applications. The worst possible approach is to allow the two applications to run in parallel and wait to see how things shape up in due course. This will never be done, and the grey area will turn into an 'information black hole' that could cause serious reputational risk to the organization.

It is important to understand the technical concepts behind SharePoint. In general, IT departments will be briefed on SP2010 by Microsoft, a systems integrator or a Microsoft Channel Partner. It is in their interests to promote SP2010 and not to highlight the product's shortcomings. That is entirely understandable, but does not help an intranet manager to appreciate the significant amount of customization that may be required. The business teams within the organization also need to be familiar with the jargon of SharePoint so that they and the IT team speak as common a language as possible.

Most WCMS applications have a major upgrade release every year, and an interim upgrade every six months. Vendors do their best to keep customers informed about the changes and enhancements that will be in the next release, and will usually have at least an outline roadmap for the next 18 months to two years. This is not Microsoft's approach. Although there have been some service packs and minor upgrades for

MOSS07 over the three-year period since its launch, SP 2010 is almost a new product as a result of some major and very welcome enhancements that have been made to the application.

SharePoint good practice

During the last few years a consensus has emerged on how to ensure that the governance of SharePoint implementations will support getting the best from its technical functionality. In general, the good practice that has been developed is common to both the 2007 and 2010 releases. A survey[3] undertaken in 2010 by the Association for Information and Image Management (AIIM) found that less than 50% of SharePoint implementations were subject to a formal business case, and only half of those required a financial justification. As a result, most did not have a management plan for which of SharePoint's many features were to be used. Meanwhile, SharePoint deployment is proceeding rapidly, with 22% of the survey respondents reporting that it was used by 100% of staff. This adoption rate is set to double over the course of 2010.

The AIIM survey also found that half of the smaller businesses implementing SharePoint were addressing the issues of information management for the first time. Even in the largest organizations, a quarter had no previous experience with enterprise content management (ECM) or document management (DM) systems. As a result, only 22% provided any guidance to staff on the use of content types and classification. In addition, just 15% had retention policies and legal discovery procedures – risking content chaos within SharePoint as well as outside it. The results of the AIIM survey are broadly in line with a survey conducted towards the end of 2009 by Eduserv[4] among universities in the UK, though at the time of the Eduserv study SP2010 had not been announced.

Planning for a SharePoint intranet implementation

When planning to use SharePoint for an intranet the following issues are among those that need to be taken into account.

Have a strategy for the development of the intranet over the next two to three years

Without a strategy it is very easy to become technology led and fail to meet short-term and long-term user requirements. Even though SharePoint, especially SP2010, has a considerably high level of functionality, that does not mean that it will meet all user requirements for the foreseeable future. With an intranet strategy in place, at least the divergence from end goals that could arise through being technology led will become more obvious to stakeholders. The process of defining business requirements has to be undertaken with the same rigour as for the purchase and implementation of a new application.

Governance needs that are to be embedded in the information management strategy

SharePoint implementations will have areas both of common interest and of conflict with many other applications, such as business intelligence, document management, search and other collaborative applications. These can only be resolved satisfactorily if the organization has an information management strategy. When departments, divisions, subsidiaries and project teams all start to find benefits in SP2010, any governance model that looks only at an individual requirement will solve the trade-off issues with other potential applications. Resources and budgets need to be prioritized, and some implementations, especially those aiming to make use of features such as a taxonomy, will need to be managed on an integrated basis.

Take special care over the management of sites

Poor site management is without doubt the area that gives rise to the most dissatisfaction with SharePoint as a collaboration application. Probably no one has put more effort into defining good practice for SharePoint collaboration applications than Michael Sampson. In his report *SharePoint Roadmap Governance Themes Workbook: site creation rights*,[5] he comments:

Making a clear decision about the rights of creating new SharePoint sites for collaboration is essential to keeping an appropriate level of control and oversight of SharePoint. Too much control and you will strangle the tool before it can be put to good use. Too little control and you will overwhelm the tool with so much junk that it becomes an unusable dumping ground where no one can find their way, or make profitable use of the tool.

He goes on to state:

Part of the signal to enforce governance is the presence or threat of chaos. If too many people are creating sites that have overlapping boundaries, that's chaos. If you are receiving complaints about the length of time required to get approval for a new site, that's chaos. If people are giving up on SharePoint and using online collaboration tools because getting a new site is 'too bureaucratic', that's chaos. Look for signals of chaos within your organization, and figure out what adjustments you need to make to remove it.

Understand training and change management requirements

Everyone involved in developing and rolling out SharePoint applications needs to understand the training and change management implications. To provide just one example, the advent of asynchronous collaboration in SP2010 opens up new possibilities, which will have to be considered as process changes, not just as a new features to be learned. The addition of the My Network feature on My Site is an example of where the benefits and implications will need to be carefully considered.

Evaluate the migration challenges very carefully

Whether the plan is to move the intranet from MOSS07 to SP2010 or to move from a current CMS to either version, the challenges of migration management will be considerable. It is easy to focus on the appearance of the desktop and feel confident that users will be able make effective use of the intranet. The problems lie more with changing the working practices for content contribution, especially where web content management is concerned. Document management, a core strength of

SharePoint, presents fewer problems because of the close integration with Office 2007 and Office 2010. As emphasized in Chapter 7, migrating content cannot begin until the configuration is stable and customization has been completed. Only then will the true scale of the migration effort become clear.

SharePoint search implementation

A particular issue with intranet deployments using SharePoint is search functionality. This was poor in MOSS07, and third-party products were often deployed to overcome the deficiencies. The search functionality with SP2010 is much improved, through the integration of technology from FAST Search into SharePoint.[6]

Table 8.1 provides a comparison of SP2010 and FAST Search Server 2010 for SharePoint,[7] based on information from Microsoft).

Table 8.1 SP2010 and FAST Search Server 2010 for SharePoint

Function	Action	SP2010	FAST Search Server 2010 for SharePoint
Basic search		Yes	Yes
Visual Best Bets	Keyword terms and synonyms defined by an administrator to enhance search results. For FAST Search Server 2010 for SharePoint only, a section of relevant information is displayed in addition to search results for a keyword term (for example, an image banner or HTML).	Limited	Yes
Scopes	Users can filter search results.	Yes	Yes
Search enhancements based on user context	Scopes Best Bets, Visual Best Bets, and document promotions and demotions to a sub-group of users.	No	Yes
Custom properties	Manages which properties are indexed and how these are treated in search results.	Yes	Yes

Continued on next page

Table 8.1 *(Continued)*

Function	Action	SP2010	FAST Search Server 2010 for SharePoint
Property extraction	Extracts key information (people names, locations, company names) from unstructured text to use as additional managed properties. (Limited: title, author and date only.)	Limited	Yes
Query federation	Federates results from multiple search sources.	Yes	Yes
Query suggestions	Provides help with query formulation, based on what the user types.	Yes	Yes
Similar results	Generates a new search based on the selected search result.	No	Yes
Sort results on managed properties or rank profiles	Sort results based on selected managed properties or by FAST Query Language (FQL) formula.	No	Yes
Relevancy tuning by document or site promotions	Promotes selected documents or sites as highly relevant results for a keyword. Demotes documents or sites to give lower rank. (Limited: promotes documents for a given site, not query specific.)	Limited	Yes
Shallow results refinement	Refines results using metadata associated with the top results.	Yes	Yes
Deep results refinement	Refines results using metadata associated with all results.	No	Yes
Previewers	Displays inline previews of Word, PowerPoint and Excel files.	No	Yes
Windows 7 federation	Enterprise search results are available in Windows desktop search.	Yes	Yes
People search	Searches used to find people by name or expertise.	Yes	Yes
Social search	Relevancy is improved by how people interact and relate with content by factoring in social tagging and the relationship of people to content and other people.	Yes	Yes
Taxonomy integration	Takes advantage of user-generated tags. Managed taxonomy influences search rankings and experience.	Yes	Yes
Multi-tenant hosting	Data partitioning of crawled data, based on tenants.	Yes	No
Rich web indexing support	Indexing of a wide variety of web content, including Flash.	No	Yes

For many intranet managers, the challenge is to decide whether to continue to use the existing search engine or to migrate not only the content but also search to SP2010.[8,9] This may mean terminating the contract with the current search vendor and investing time in learning how to get the best from the Microsoft search functions.

Resources

1   The Intranet Benchmarking Forum published *The SharePoint 2010 Intranet*, which sets out the main features of SharePoint 2010 from the viewpoint of an intranet manager:
    https://ibforum.site-ym.com/store/view_product.asp?id=525660.

2   Every year the Nielsen Norman Group publish *Intranet Design Annual*:
    www.nngroup.com/reports/intranet/design/.

3   www.AIIM.org. AIIM also publishes surveys and reports on SharePoint adoption:
    www.aiim.org/sharepoint.

4   The Eduserv report on the use of SharePoint in (UK) higher education can be downloaded from:
    www.eduserv.org.uk/news/2010/sharepoint-in-he-final-report.aspx.

5   Sampson, M. (2010) *SharePoint Roadmap Governance Themes Workbook: site creation rights*, www.michaelsampson.net/sharepointroadmap.html.

6   Bennett, M., Fried, J., Kehoe, M., and Voskresenskaya, N. (2010) *Professional Microsoft Search: FAST Search, SharePoint Search, and Search Server*, Wrox, www.wrox.com.

7   http://sharepoint.microsoft.com/en-us/product/capabilities/search/Pages/default.aspx.

8   SharePoint implementation and product development is monitored by the Real Story Group:
    www.realstorygroup.com.

9   Jamison, S., Hanley, S., and Cardarelli, M. (2010) *Essential SharePoint*, Addison-Wesley, www.informit.com/mstechseries, is a good non-technical introduction to SharePoint 2010.

Part 3
Operational planning

9

Establishing the intranet team

Introduction

There is now good evidence from both the report *Global Intranet Trends*[1] and from the work of the Nielsen Norman Group that, ideally, there should be one full-time intranet manager for every 3000 users of the intranet. Most organizations would see this as an unattainable and unrealistic target at a time when they are making efforts to reduce employee numbers in an attempt to reduce costs. However, these organizations fail to recognize not only the role that the intranet manager plays in ensuring that the intranet is fit for purpose, but also that there is a distinct role of 'intranet manager'. Indeed, in many organizations the 'intranet manager' may well have additional tasks and a job title that does not reflect the work they do in managing the intranet.

It does not help that there is no professional organization to represent intranet managers, there is no structured training for intranet managers that would lead to some form of certification, and there is no obvious career path for an intranet manager. If the numbers of people with intranet management roles were small, this might be an acceptable situation, but the reality is different. In the UK, CILIP: the Chartered Institute of Library and Information Professionals, has a membership of around 20,000. With at least 50,000 intranets in the UK it is quite possible that there are more intranet managers (either full time or part time) than there are information professionals. The situation is probably similar in many other countries. Even in the USA there is no association for intranet professionals.

Hopefully, this situation will change. Certainly the advent of many informal groups of intranet managers is helping to establish good practice, and from their meetings intranet managers are able to gain ideas that they can use in their own organizations. From my attendance at these meetings, it is clear that many intranet managers tend to find themselves in their posts almost by accident. When a vacancy occurred they just happened to be able to take on the responsibility, and now enjoy the work that the position requires. However, many are now wondering how to develop their careers. Moving to another organization is certainly a possibility, but the new employer has to take on trust their skills in intranet management and will almost certainly not be able to look at the intranet of their current employer and judge for themselves, in the way that they might assess a web manager.

A question of title

Jane McConnell has published a very useful analysis of the range of job titles held by the respondents to her *Global Intranet Trends Report 2007*.[2] They are summarized in Table 9.1.

This is a very useful analysis because it highlights that the role and positioning of the intranet manager reflects the way in which the organization sees the intranet, and also what it regards as the important characteristics of the intranet. It also depends on the roles available to the department that is taking responsibility for the intranet.

Table 9.1 Intranet manager job titles	
Respondent	**Job title**
'My role is focused on the intranet'	Intranet Co-ordinator Intranet Manager Intranet Leader Intranet Gatekeeper Intranet Overseer
'I am in charge of content'	Intranet Producer Intranet Content Management Editorial Webmaster – Internet – Intranet – E-communications
'We are here to serve'	Director, Intranet Services Interactive Communications Manager IT Manager: Communication – Collaboration Intranet Team, Internal and Change Communications Online Communications Officer Internet and Intranet Support Team Leader Global Intranet Services Manager Manager, Enterprise Web Management
'The intranet is important'	Vice President Intranet Services Corporate Communications: Program Manager, Intranet Strategy and Production Global Intranet Specialist
'The intranet brings business value to the organisation'	Internal Web Capability Business Consultant | Web Strategy and Marketing Intranet Business Analyst Business Change Manager – Intranet
'Beyond the intranet'	Director, Workplace Strategy and Enablement: Total Workplace Experience Community of Excellence

The role of the intranet team

Even in situations where the intranet manager is not able to devote all their time to the intranet there will still be an intranet team, because the support and skills of this team are a vital element of the service being provided to the organization. A very good and concise list of the responsibilities of an intranet team has been developed by James Robertson:[3]

- managing the intranet home page
- structuring the top levels of the site
- promoting the use of the intranet
- determining the overall intranet strategy
- establishing policies and governance
- reviewing pages published by business areas

- supporting intranet authors and publishers
- liaising with intranet stakeholders
- managing key technologies, such as the CMS and search engine
- conducting intranet improvement projects.

In my view, missing from this list are:

- maintaining an awareness of good intranet practice
- assessing usability and accessibility
- working with those responsible for related applications
- ensuring that the intranet meets internal and external compliance requirements.

These responsibilities can be very time consuming to perform. Good examples include reviewing pages published by business areas, and managing the search application. In the case of the former, the review process may highlight the need for content contributor training; and in the latter case the time needed to analyse search logs is always underestimated.

Moreover, these are tasks that have to be performed on a regular basis. In addition, it may well be necessary to specify and select new CMS and search applications, or to undertake a major redesign of the intranet. Given the scale and range of these tasks, the emerging standard of one manager for every 3000 users actually seems a very conservative requirement.

Skills for intranet management

Global Intranet Trends Report 2008[1] included questions about the knowledge base of the respondents, most of whom will come from fairly large organizations. The skill areas that respondents considered to be important were (in descending order of priority):

- user-centred approach, design
- information architecture (structuring information)
- organizational dynamics
- business and business processes

- tools, e.g. search, content management systems
- technology trends
- needs analysis techniques
- business cases
- finances, ROI analysis.

By any standard, that is a very wide range of skill areas! For those who possess some or all of these skills, the role of intranet manager can be very fulfilling, and certainly has the potential to have an impact on the operational performance of the organization in a way that few other roles would have, outside the senior management team.

For those who have not gained this breadth of experience through their educational and career paths, acquiring these skills through on-the-job development is very challenging. There are no continuing professional development programmes available, remarkably few conferences, very few books and reports, and just a few communities of practice. A review of the information management courses provided by the major information schools in the USA and the UK shows a disconcerting lack of course content on intranet design and management, despite the potential market for these skills.

A significant development in 2010 was the establishment by Mark Morell,[4] intranet manager at BT, of a LinkedIn group on intranet career path development. This arose from a very insightful post that Morrell published on his blog. One of the initial areas of discussion was the top three skills that an intranet manager needed to have. Morell suggested that these were:

Strategic – The ability to develop a strategy that aligns with the organization's and execute it.

Communications – The ability to build relationships with people across the organization – stakeholders, IT partners, publishers and users. That needs a great ability to talk the right language with the right people and engage them to help you implement your plan.

Project management – A plan is no good unless it is properly managed so that you have the right priorities, focus and time scales, and the ability to change if circumstances demand it.

This stimulated a lot of discussion, leading to the following additions to this list:

- building relationships
- commercial awareness
- creative problem solving
- creativity
- driving change
- empathy
- holistic thinking
- influencing
- leadership
- sales.

Helpful though these suggestions are, many companies are faced with developing a job description for an intranet manager and just to include a list of skills is only part of the solution.

Job descriptions for intranet managers

Every organization has its own format for setting out job descriptions. The description in Example 9.1 comes from a major multinational company seeking to recruit an experienced intranet manager.

....

EXAMPLE 9.1 Global Intranet Manager – job description

Scope

The Global Intranet Manager is responsible to the Intranet Strategy Board for ensuring that the company's intranet meets the requirements of users for trustworthy information to support the development of the business and also their own career development. This will require building close working relationships with a wide range of stakeholders throughout the company.

The Global Intranet Manager will chair the Intranet Operations Group and will have budget responsibility for all aspects of intranet operations, including content publishing, information architecture, service performance (in co-operation with the corporate IT department), training and support.

The Global Intranet Manager will liaise closely with managers of other business applications, such as corporate website, e-learning, social media and customer relationship management, to ensure that the intranet is positioned as a complementary application.

The company is going through a period of rapid business expansion and it is essential that the Global Intranet Manager not only ensures that the intranet meets current requirements but also works proactively to develop intranet content and applications to support emerging business requirements.

Key accountabilities

- Develop an annual operational plan for the development of the intranet that is in line with the strategic and operational requirements of the business.
- Identify and report on appropriate KPIs that indicate the level to which employees trust and use the information on the intranet.
- Develop and implement a governance policy for the intranet.
- Develop good relationships with managers of other business applications that currently or potentially complement the intranet and from these identify and achieve integrated solutions that meet business requirements.
- Develop and provide training courses, training material and help desk provision for both users and content contributors to the intranet.
- Identify, evaluate, justify and integrate into the intranet external web-based information resources.
- Maintain excellent relationships with internal and external providers of hardware, software and other services to ensure high availability of the intranet and effective operation.
- Devise and conduct periodic usability surveys.
- Monitor user satisfaction and report on actions being taken to meet emerging user requirements.
- Monitor developments in intranet good practice and where appropriate introduce these into the intranet.
- Work closely and co-operatively with staff around the world with responsibilities for intranet content publishing and local intranet support.

Key competencies
- experience in managing an intranet
- experience in using content management and search software applications for either intranet and/or websites
- experience in conducting user requirements and usability reviews
- experience in project management.

Key traits
- ability to achieve a consensus of views and priorities of stakeholders
- ability to build excellent relationships with employees worldwide at all management levels
- familiarity with the technology of content management and search applications
- effective presentation and communication skills.

....

Although all these requirements are very sound ones, the most important is missing, and that is an understanding of how the business works, which can take a considerable amount of time to discover. When I look at my own work as an intranet consultant one of the key competencies that I can bring to the service of my clients is a very diverse career path, much of it in the consultancy business, giving me the opportunity to find out at least something about the organizational and cultural dynamics of organizations. Much of my work is with multinational organizations and, having worked on projects in over 30 countries, I hope that I am at least aware of potential cultural and linguistic challenges.

There is also a market for contract intranet managers, usually to guide an organization through a period of change. The requirements of one such position in the UK in August 2010 were as set out in Example 9.2.

....
EXAMPLE 9.2 Interim Intranet Manager – job description

We are in the process of redesigning and redeveloping our Group intranet as a major internal communication channel using SharePoint as the content management platform. We are now seeking an Interim Intranet Manager to work closely with our IT specialists and Internal

Communications teams to focus on the development, implementation and establishment of the new corporate intranet as the key internal communications channel within our business.

You will already have acted as an intranet champion for a large business and ideally have worked on intranet redevelopment projects involving migration of content.

You will have full editorial control over intranet content and in addition you will oversee intranet governance policies.

You will also contribute to the overall look and feel of the design of the site and coach other internal publishers/contributors in editorial and writing and publishing techniques.

We are looking for someone who is able to apply new thinking, ideas and techniques to the corporate intranet to ensure that it is engaging and a place that people want to visit.

You will have very strong communication skills with the ability to write plainly and engagingly and be able to present material clearly for large audiences of all types, from shop floor to senior management.

Technically you should be conversant with SharePoint and have understanding of, and experience in, corporate intranets, writing and designing pages, intranet architecture and platforms.

This interim role is initially for 6 months but could lead to a more permanent role with a negotiable salary depending on experience.

••

This is a very good summary of what is involved in being an intranet manager – but to achieve a redevelopment on SharePoint in six months is probably verging on the unrealistic.

The wider intranet team

In reality, the intranet team is much larger and more diverse than just the intranet manager, or even the global intranet management team. Content contributors are also members of the team, for without their work the intranet would not exist. The list of contributors also needs to include staff adding user-generated comment in the form of blogs and comments on published content. All these content contributors need to be supported, trained, encouraged and occasionally admonished. The introduction of social media applications may result in a doubling of the number of content contributors and an increase in the intranet team's workload.

Staff contributing content to the intranet should have their work recognized in their job descriptions. Content contribution cannot be a hobby. It takes time to adapt existing content (perhaps a project report) for intranet use, adding an HTML summary to a Word or PDF document, adding metadata, as well as being responsible for future reviewing and revision of the document. Sadly, the managers of content contributors sometimes fail to recognize that the information being added to the intranet may not be just for the use of the department itself and could well be of value to a substantial number of employees throughout the organization. Without an appropriate level of support from a manager, a content contributor will not spend the time required to present the content in the most appropriate way. The result will be that someone will take the content, trust it, and then make a decision that turns out to be inappropriate because of lack of quality in the base information.

The role of the HR department

HR departments usually make good and extensive use of an intranet for the publication of polices and for a range of employee self-service applications. In relation to the intranet, HR has another vital role, and that is to ensure that:

- there is a current and realistic job description for intranet managers
- the salary is in line with the value that the intranet manager is adding to the organization, and takes into account the replacement cost of an external appointment should they leave
- training requirements arising from the job description and the responsibilities of the intranet manager are identified and supported
- the career development of the intranet manager is carefully considered, as there may not be any obvious development routes within the organization

- the intranet manager's role is identified as one where the organization could be at risk, should the manager leave
- the tasks of content contributors are included in their job descriptions
- given the broad range of responsibilities of an intranet manager, a senior manager is appointed as their mentor. This is essential in the case of an intranet manager joining the organization.

Over the next few years the impact of social media and collaboration applications, in particular, will change the balance of the work of the intranet manager. Job descriptions certainly need to be reviewed so as to take account of these changes, but the most important role of HR is to ensure that the person to whom the intranet manager reports, and indeed the manager at the level above, understands explicitly the skills, roles and responsibilities needed to ensure that the intranet is able to meet current requirements and to respond quickly to emerging requirements.

Resources

1   *Global Intranet Trends* reports at: http://netjmc.com.
2   Jane McConnell's commentary on job titles for intranet managers can be found at: http://netjmc.com/future-intranet/intranet-manager/does-your-job-title-reflect-the-strategy-and-vision-behind-your-role.
3   *What Every Intranet Team Should Know* is written by James Robertson and published by Step Two Designs: www.steptwo.com.au.
4   Mark Morrell's discussion on these issues can be found at: http://markmorrell.wordpress.com/2010/06/03/whats-an-intranet-managers-career-path/.

10
Managing intranet projects

Creating an operational plan for an intranet

The definitive approach to intranet development is the 6 × 2 methodology developed by James Robertson of Step Two Designs.[1] At the heart of the 6 × 2 methodology is a focus on the coming six months. Rather than just steadily working on longer-term activities, this approach asks: what can be delivered in the next six months? The focus is placed on identifying concrete deliverables that benefit the organization, rather than on activities that only prepare for future improvements or address behind-the-scenes issues. In this way, activities are identified that will have the greatest impact on the intranet and on the intranet team. This is, in effect, the use of 'agile' project management, with a time box of six months.

Detailed project planning is used to ensure that the selected items are actually achievable, and that a clear sequence of activities is defined. The possible activities for the following six months are also sketched out (thus the 6 × 2 name), giving the intranet team a roadmap for the year ahead. All of this is then used to create a compelling briefing for senior management, as well as a communications message for the wider organization.

This is a cyclical process, with each six-month period of activity leading into the next. Underlying this is a steady build-up of momentum for the intranet, giving an 'upwards spiral' that allows more to be done in each six-month period. In this way, the intranet team can steadily work on ever-larger needs and issues, even when the starting point is extremely constrained. It no longer needs to wait for the 'right conditions' to arise – instead, the team can act constructively and proactively to build an increasingly effective intranet.

One of the key principles behind this approach to intranet planning is to focus on delivering new functionality and content. One very practical way of ensuring that the intranet is steadily moving forward in its capabilities is to give the site a version number. Start by giving the current intranet a version number. While necessarily somewhat arbitrary, this version number will define a starting point from which to measure future improvements. The following version numbers could be used:

- Version 1.0, if the intranet has been recently launched
- Version 2.0 or 3.0, if the intranet is well established
- Version 4.0 (or higher), if the intranet is mature and moving towards the next stage of its evolution.

One of the benefits of this approach is that IT managers understand the concept of what are often referred to as 'dot releases'. In addition, by posting the version number on the home page of the intranet, the intranet team has a hook for promoting site changes that otherwise might well be invisible to most users if an incremental approach were taken. The final benefit is that it enables dependencies to be defined. For example, upgrading the staff directory might be a proposed Version 2.5 release, but this release can only take place after the IT department has integrated all the AD directories into Version 2.4.1 and HR has set out a policy on the use of staff photographs in Version 2.4.2.

Project management

Implementing an operational plan is almost always a series of projects and not 'business as usual'. This is because it is very rare for any step in intranet development to be undertaken without balancing the requirements of multiple stakeholders against the limited resources so often allocated to the intranet. This means that good project management is essential for achieving intranet user requirements, as a balance needs to be kept between meeting these requirements and the resources (time and people) that are available.

Too many organizations decide that (for example) specifying a search engine or creating a new home page design is indeed a project, go ahead to appoint a project leader who has had no formal training in project management, and a project team, and then sit back in the absolute expectation that all will now go according to plan.

This chapter provides no more than an introduction to project management, primarily to illustrate that there are various ways of managing projects and to highlight some of the problems that can arise. Even if there is a substantial amount of software development involved, using someone with a background in IT project management is unlikely to be effective.[2,3]

The primary requirements for anyone managing an intranet project are:

- knowledge of the organization, and how it operates
- a good network of contacts at most locations and management levels
- the trust of stakeholders
- understanding of the difference between 'fitness for purpose' and 'fitness to specification'.

The speed with which business and user requirements may change means that any project based on the achievement of a documented specification is more likely to fail than to succeed.

Project life-cycle management

There are a number of approaches to managing a project from inception to delivery, and each has a place in intranet development.

Serial life cycle, also referred to as Waterfall or Phase-Gate

A serial project life cycle works well when, right from the beginning, there is a very clear final deliverable and each step of the project can be clearly defined at the outset. This works well with the implementation of a new CMS application:

- requirements definition
- RFP (aka invitation to tender)
- evaluation
- contract agreement
- installation
- configuration and customization
- test and acceptance of the software
- content migration
- usability testing
- release.

There are some other sub-steps, but these are the main elements of the project and there are clear deliverables at each major stage. Many organizations are comfortable with this approach because they feel in control of the progress of the project through reports of deliverables against schedule and costs against budget. In practice, this approach only works at all well when the project timetable is fairly short (perhaps no more than a couple of months) and when relatively few people are involved. Using Microsoft Project is not a solution to effective project management, and few people are sufficiently adept at using Microsoft Project to use it effectively after it has been set up.

The major risk will be that the requirements are not challenged during the course of the project. The longer the project, the greater the chance that this will happen; and the more detailed the list of requirements, the more likely it is that many will be found to be irrelevant as the project draws to a close. Finally, because the process is linear, once one deliverable date has been missed there is usually no slack time available to get back on schedule. It is a brave project manager who states up front that they have built three weeks of slack to accommodate overruns, as it then looks as though they do not have control of the project.

Iterative life cycle

In an iterative life cycle the underlying principle is to work on a number of individual elements at the same time, each of which is developed to a defined stage and tested. All the elements are then included in a final integration, test and launch period. For an intranet, the development of a new home page might be a good example, and some of the individual elements might be:

- creating new design templates
- developing a presentation of the time and weather in major office locations
- selecting and integrating an external news clipping service
- upgrading the staff directory to give a better search experience.

All of these can be progressed in parallel but need to come together at a time when it is still possible to make changes to some or all of them and to other elements, when the results of the usability tests on the new home page are available. This approach enables changes in the requirements for an individual element to be accommodated during the development process.

One of the risks of this approach is that it can be a challenge to decide which elements to work on first, assuming that there are only limited development resources. Some teams will want to tackle the most risky elements first, so as to get them out of the way, whereas there may be pressure to develop those elements with the greatest visual impact, so as to impress the sponsors. Iterative projects are also likely to need a full-time project manager, especially when one developer may be working on more than one element and is under pressure from each of the development teams to spend more time with its own element than with those of the other teams.

Agile life cycle

An agile life cycle is based on very short periods of development, perhaps only a week, where the customer (the intranet manager) is very close to the work of the development teams. The objective is to build and show something within a very tight schedule that is then releasable to the intranet community. Project scheduling is turned on its head. The question is not how long it will take to develop something, but what can be delivered in a week that moves the overall project forward. For an intranet one example might be the development of an e-expenses form. This might start off with the creation of a paper version that must be signed off, and then develop the functionality to provide electronic sign-off – which could be dependent on whether the expenses are in a single currency or in multiple currencies for which exchange rates need to be determined.

There are endless variations of these three basic approaches, and none is better than the other. The reason for setting them out here is to ensure that intranet teams are aware of the options and start to take project management seriously. IT departments will often have their own favourite approaches, and unless both the intranet and IT teams make the selection and adoption of an agreed project management methodology an initial requirement of the project, the chances of success will be low. This is especially the case where development and intranet teams are not co-located. When the SharePoint team is in California and the intranet team is Frankfurt, nine time zones ahead, an experienced project manager is essential, as well as agreement on date formats that are unambiguous. A date expressed as 3/5/10 could be 3 May 2010 or 5 March 2010, and that could make quite a difference to meeting the project deadlines.

PRINCE2 project management

One of the most widely used project management methodologies is PRINCE2 (Projects In Controlled Environments), which was first released by the UK government in 1989. It is now widely used worldwide, and many are courses available through which project managers can be certified in the use of PRINCE2. It does not specify any particular project life-cycle methodology and is probably most useful for serial projects.

The emphasis in PRINCE2 is on the development of a sound business case at the outset of the project, along with excellent project communication and a strong commitment to quality. The PRINCE2 manual runs to over 400 pages, and without adequate training its adoption for intranet management will bring a false degree of comfort to senior managers. Adopting PRINCE2 is not an automatic guarantee of project success.

Defining the responsibility of the project manager

Something that is often overlooked is the need for a well-defined set of responsibilities for the project manager. This person will often also be the intranet manager; whenever someone has dual roles it is essential that these are clearly set out. The responsibilities typically include the following:

- archiving documents and other deliverables created by the project
- ensuring that staff working on the project have appropriate skills, expertise and training
- maintaining a risk register
- making effective use of staff working on the project
- planning ahead for staff not being available, due to vacations or other projects
- planning, organizing and reporting on meetings
- reporting on the project schedule and project costs
- reviewing the forecast project schedule
- setting up and implementing a quality management process for deliverables.

That is quite a substantial list of tasks for an individual project, and it is not unusual to find a number of projects being undertaken simultaneously. This is where good direction from an intranet steering group becomes so important, as the person to whom the intranet manager reports may well not be able to see the total picture and, without this perspective, may impose priorities on the intranet manager that may not be in the best interests of the organization.

The role of a project manager is not something that can be ignored just because the organization has invested in a collaboration application. Collaboration is only one aspect of effective project management.

Table 10.1 Core elements of the project initiation document	
Element	**Description**
1. Project definition	This sets out what the project is to achieve, and should do so in such a way that the end point is clearly defined.
2. Business case	The business case for starting the project should already have been agreed and signed off, so this will be a short section to set the project in context.
3. Project approach	This section is a synopsis of how the project will be undertaken, which might involve some user research to begin with, then the development of a proof of concept, followed by usability tests. In small projects the quality plan could be included in this section.
4. Project plan	The schedule for the project should be set out, highlighting any dependencies with other projects, and the major review points.
5. Project organization	Project team members will be listed, together with their roles and responsibilities and the amount of time they will be spending on the project. The membership of the project board should be included.
6. Project budget	The format of this section will depend on whether it is necessary to specify and cross-charge time incurred by staff on secondment from other departments or subsidiaries.
7. Risks	This is a very important section of the PID. It should list not only the risks but also the ways in which they will be identified, quantified and managed.
8. Controls	These are the standard reports that will be presented to track the progress of the project.
9. Communication plan	All the stakeholders need to be kept informed of the progress of the project, even if they do not see the standard reports.

Project initiation document

No matter how large or small the project, drawing up the project initiation document (PID) is the first step. This might be a only page or two long, or it could be ten times that length. Table 10.1 lists the core elements of the PID.

This PID is the baseline for the project, and any changes to it should be signed off by the project board.

Project completion

At the end of the project one of the responsibilities of the project manager should be to synthesize the outcomes of the project in terms of experience that will help future project managers and project teams. The project board should not sign off the project as being completed until the record of 'lessons learned' had been completed and filed.

Resources

1   James Robertson of Step Two Designs has written a report on a project methodology for intranet development:
    www.steptwo.com.au/products/6x2.

2   Lientz, B. P and Larssen, L. (2006) *Risk Management for IT Projects*, London: Butterworth-Heinemann.

3   Rothman, J. (2007) *Manage It! Your guide to pragmatic project management*, Rayleigh, NC: The Pragmatic Bookshelf.

11
Evaluating risks

Introduction

The value of using a risk management approach to building a business case has already been covered in Chapter 3. There is an equal value in building a risk register for the intranet itself as a means of managing both opportunities and problems. At the core of risk management is a means of quantifying the risk.[1] A risk (e.g. the intranet manager leaving) is scored on Impact × Probability. Of these two parameters, Probability is much more difficult than Impact to assess objectively, so concern should be focused on risks that have a high impact, as the organization will be put at risk whenever they occur.

Risk is generally scored on a scale of 1 to 5 and the scores are plotted on a 5 × 5 matrix, as illustrated in Figure 11.1.

Some possible impact parameters are:

1 Restricted to a single department for a short period of time.
2 Affects more than one department/business unit.
3 Has significant impact on the operations of more than one department/business unit.

4   Affects operations throughout the organization.
5   Could bring the organization into disrepute through a failure to meet stakeholder obligations.

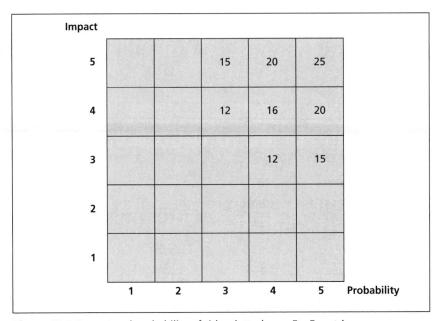

Figure 11.1 Impact and probability of risks plotted on a 5 x 5 matrix

Probability parameters might be:

1   Likely to occur within the next two years.
2   Likely to occur within the next twelve months.
3   Likely to occur within the next six months.
4   Likely to occur at any time with one month or less of advance warning.
5   Likely to occur with minimal advance warning.

Some organizations feel that using a scale of 1 to 3 is adequate. It is probably better to begin by using the more detailed 5 × 5 approach and then see if a 1 to 3 range is in fact adequate to set out the risks.

As with the risk scales, there are different approaches to recording the elements of the risk register. Figure 11.2 illustrates one possible approach. Many larger organizations will have corporate formats for risk registers and, where possible, these should be adopted.

Condition	Risk
If this happens	The intranet sponsor changes corporate roles or leaves the company, so there is no corporate sponsor for the intranet.
Then the impact will be	Plans to enhance the intranet might be delayed, pending a new sponsor being agreed, or could be changed if the new sponsor had a different perspective.
Impact	4
Probability	4
This risk will be managed by	Identifying potential sponsors from among current senior managers and/or appointing a deputy sponsor.
If we can achieve this then the scores would be	—
Impact	2
Probability	1

Figure 11.2 Risk register entry example

Potential risks for intranet operations

In my consulting work, early in the initial engagement meeting I ask the intranet manager for a list of the potential risks they have to manage, and it can be revealing to find out how little attention has been paid to identifying and evaluating operational risks. The list in Table 11.1 is by no means a definitive one, as risks depend on the context of an individual organization. For each of these risks an intranet manager should be able to quantify the impact and have a Plan B to mitigate the risk, even if working out a probability score is perhaps not worth the effort.

Some possible solutions to the risks in Table 11.1 are shown for the purposes of illustration. The solutions will, of course, need to be tailored to the organization.

Table 11.1 Risk responses

People

Risk	Response
Intranet sponsor is not able to continue to provide sponsorship	Try to ensure that the governance processes are strong enough that progress does not depend on the work of one person at a senior level.
Intranet sponsor does not take an active and supportive role	Work with the sponsor to develop a scope note for them so that they know from the outset what the role will entail.
Intranet manager leaves the organization, or is no longer able to take responsibility for the intranet	Build some scenarios of possible solutions, perhaps with the web manager taking on a dual role, or bringing someone in on a contract basis until a staff appointment can be made.
Core intranet operation roles cannot be included in job descriptions	Obtain examples of how the process is managed in other organizations. Often the problem is that HR does not know where to begin the process.
Intranet team is too small to provide adequate support to the intranet	Set out clearly the user requirements that have been established, highlighting the ones that very closely support business performance, and discuss with stakeholders which of these requirements can be ignored, setting out in neutral terms what the impact on the organization could be.

Content

Risk	Response
As a result of poor information quality a poor decision was made	Ensure that all content contributors not only have initial training but also are monitored by the intranet team to see if additional training may be required. Recording the name of the contributor at the bottom of the page increases the sense of responsibility and exposure of the content contributor.
Important content is held on the intranet but cannot be found easily using the search engine	The intranet team should be familiar with the main types of search that are being carried out, and should run them from time to time to ensure that the results on the first page really are of high relevance. Search logs should be reviewed regularly to spot emerging problems. Best Bets solutions would place important policies and applications in the header of the first page of results.
Important content has not been added to the intranet because a content contributor had to cope with more important tasks	If an individual staff member's responsibilities for content contribution are not included in a job description, this is a fundamental breach of good governance and should be referred up to the intranet steering group for action.

Continued on next page

Table 11.1 (Continued)	
Technology	
Risk	**Response**
CMS/search vendor is taken over and future support for the incumbent CMS/search is open to question	Stay very close to the vendor so that the customer support staff feel a strong sense of responsibility to ensure that the organization is kept fully in the picture about future plans.
IT department imposes SharePoint without taking into account intranet requirements	The intranet team should maintain a document that sets out the impact and opportunity for SharePoint. Rarely is this a decision that can be overturned by edict, but IT managers want a successful implementation and usually welcome constructive support from the intranet team.
Internal development resources are not adequate to support the intranet strategy	With a good business plan and excellent communications this scenario should have a very low probability.
IT is outsourced without the impact on intranet operations being assessed	This could well be the case with a move to cloud computing. This situation is one that should be anticipated by the intranet team, to the extent of circulating a brief report on the benefits and opportunities.
Disaster recovery procedures do not take into account intranet requirements	This situation is probably counter to IT governance, and should be brought to the notice of the most senior IT manager, highlighting the potential impacts on business continuity.
Information	
Risk	**Response**
Confidential information is surfaced in the intranet, especially through a search	The information security model should ensure that this is a rare occurrence, but when it does happen there should be a feedback box so that an employee can alert the intranet team, who will then treat the problem with an appropriate level of urgency.
Decision is made on the basis of information that is in fact no longer current and accurate	A modern CMS provides a wide range of options that ensure that content is subject to review on an appropriate basis. The problem often arises when an employee has left the organization and the internal procedures are not adequate to notify the intranet team and the department manager of the loss of a content contributor so that a handover can be arranged.
Inappropriate content is posted on a social media application on the intranet	A feedback box that facilitates peer review will help address this issue, as will a prominent notice about breach of trust. Naming the person concerned is not helpful; it is enough that everyone knows that there are mechanisms for dealing with such a situation.

The success of any programme of risk management depends on all concerned accepting that business risks cannot be reduced to zero. Developing a risk register is a fundamental task in any organization and the intranet should follow suit and, if possible, be an exemplar of best practice. There is much to be gained from publishing the risk register on the intranet so as to reassure employees that considerable care is being taken to maintain trust in and access to the intranet.

Resource

1   http://en.wikipedia.org/wiki/Risk_managment.

12
Conforming to compliance requirements

Introduction

Intranet managers need to be conversant with a number of compliance matters where ignorance of local and international legislation and regulation is not acceptable as a defence. The commentary on these topics provided in this chapter should be regarded as being for the purposes of illustration only. Legal advice should be sought for the specific jurisdiction in which the intranet is being operated.

Records retention policy

A 'record' is evidence of an activity or decision and demonstrates accountability. It is not possible to define a record in terms of a particular category of documents, or by the age of the item. A comment in a blog or on a wiki could indicate that an action has taken place, and so becomes a record of that event having occurred. The use of social media in this example is deliberate: in the world of records management there is no such thing as a distinction between 'formal' and 'informal' content.

A 'controlled document' is one in which the revision history is important, such that employees need to be aware of which version (not always the latest version) they should be using.

It is important to distinguish between 'records' and 'archives'. A record has a limited and defined life, which may range from seven years, in the case of financial records, to five years after the withdrawal of a product from the market. An archive is a collection of records that have a long-term and often indeterminate life. All too often the terms 'record' and 'archive' are used synonymously, which is incorrect.

The issue about the extent to which information that is available on an intranet needs to be regarded as a corporate record is often overlooked because of a concern about the sheer volume of the content and the range of file formats involved. Often a document management system is used to manage corporate records, but such a system will rarely be used for the entire intranet, collaboration spaces and social media messages.

Increasingly, videos are used to illustrate the way in which particular activities should be performed – for example, using a forklift truck to load a vehicle. In due course the video might be updated and the previous version deleted so that the 'correct' version is available on the intranet. But let us suppose that some years later a warehouse employee suffers from a back ailment that they claim was caused by the presentation of inadequate information in training the video. When the organization has to defend itself, can the specific version of the video be found? Inability to locate the video might be used by the prosecution as evidence that the information was indeed inadequate and the reason why the video was deleted.

It is especially important to manage situations such as this in the USA, where federal e-discovery rules can bring an intranet centre-stage in any Federal action. Where an organization does not have a records manager, it is essential to take advice from a records management consultant working with the organization's legal and risk managers.

Information security

All organizations process information that is sensitive or confidential. Such information needs to be held securely and not disclosed to unauthorized personnel. It is also required to be held in such a way that it is available in a timely manner and is protected against deliberate or inadvertent alteration. These requirements are summarized as the three key parameters of information security:

Confidentiality – protecting sensitive information from unauthorized disclosure
Integrity – safeguarding the accuracy and completeness of information
Availability – ensuring that information is available when it is required.

Over the last few years issues of information security have started to rise up the list of corporate risks. Much of the attention of IT managers and information security professionals has been on making sure that information generated by their organization remains behind the firewall. IT managers are well aware of the problems created by a wide range of IT hardware and software – ranging from wireless routers to high-capacity flash drives – and of attempts by hackers to break in to databases containing confidential and business-critical information. Even within an organization there will be well tested authentication procedures to ensure that only authorized staff are able to either read, or read and modify, content in databases such as those maintained by financial, operations and HR departments.

However, far less attention has been paid to implementing procedures to ensure that confidential information in documents is appropriately protected. Many organizations still provide little guidance for staff on the management of documents containing confidential information, or even a clear definition of what constitutes 'confidential information'. The extent to which information is confidential may change over time, and with the role of the employee in the organization. E-mail circulation lists are probably heavily relied on to restrict the distribution of documents to named individuals, but in our experience security labelling of documents is inconsistent, or at best only the cover page is so labelled, and not the individual pages of a document or spreadsheet. To remove a watermark from an MS Office document is as simple as it was to add it in the first place.

Given the number of documents residing on any server, the chances of a member of staff finding confidential information are probably very remote if they are working via a folder structure or a listing of documents by title. The challenge comes when a search application is implemented. Unless the circulation and security permissions related to a document are identifiable by the indexing engine, as the search application builds the initial index the document will become open access. Whatever search engine you are currently using, it can be instructive to search on the term 'confidential' and look through the results. It could well be that many of the hits are guidance notes on how to manage confidential information – but can you be certain that this is the case for all the documents listed? Just one document containing information that, if widely circulated by a disaffected member of staff or a temporary worker, could impact on the operations and reputation of your organization is one document too many.

Data privacy

A substantial challenge for those working with intranets is how to ensure compliance with data privacy legislation, especially if the organization is subject to EU legislation, which extends to anyone from any country who is working in the EU. The problems of conformance are not just related to intranets. The same issues apply to e-mails and any other form of transferring data, such as by a flash drive, or in a laptop computer being taken out of the country. For example, sending details of an employee's CV to the USA from the UK without consent could be in breach of the legislation. There is a view taken by some companies that if they only send information to other sites of their company then the legislation does not apply. This is not the case, and full consent needs to be obtained.

This is because there is also a very important distinction between personal information and sensitive personal information in EU legislation.

Sensitive personal information covers:

- the racial or ethnic origin of the data subject
- their political opinions
- their religious beliefs or other beliefs of a similar nature
- whether they are a member of a trade union
- their physical or mental health or condition
- their sexual life
- the commission or alleged commission by them of any offence.

One of the key issues is that a person has to give their informed consent for this information to be held in a database. To develop a scenario, let us assume that the HR database of a US organization in Europe contains, with permission, information on the racial or ethnic origin of staff. Let us assume also that someone in the USA wants to check on which members of staff had a particular ethnic origin. The first issue is whether data privacy legislation would allow anyone in the USA to carry out that search, which might well require authorization under the Safe Harbor protocols. If such authorization has not been given, the search logs, in revealing the search, could potentially put the search team under a requirement to inform the organization that such a search had been carried out.

It has to be understood that this is a hypothetical scenario, and is included only to highlight the complexities of data privacy legislation and the fact that, to date, search logs have probably escaped due attention.

Some intranets have an internal staff newsletter. In the interests of good communication there might, for instance, be a news story about how a member of staff had been ill, but was now coming back to work for a few days a week. This could be regarded as sensitive personal data, as it relates to the health of the person, and this should not then be circulated electronically without the permission of the person concerned.

It would certainly seem that individual employees will need to be issued with some form of amendment to their contract of employment which states what personal information is being sent (either by push or through pull) to other countries, and for what purpose, and their consent sought for this transfer. This will certainly apply to any CVs that contain personal information such as date of birth, sex, home address, or any information on religious beliefs, etc.

Indeed, one of the problems is working out just what is covered by the Directive, and advice will need to be taken from lawyers specializing in data privacy, recognizing that there is no case law at the present moment, and that in each country the data protection regulator, who is independent of the government, may take a different view on what is acceptable, especially in the early stages of the implementation of the Directive. At this time it seems unlikely that a generic clause that allows the company to send personal information around to any of its sites worldwide for 'management purposes' would be permitted under the provisions of the Directive.

Many consulting projects, especially in human resources and change management, may require the consultants to check on personal information about employees. Using a corporate intranet from a single site to gain access to this information is likely to be forbidden, and of course if this information is to be held by a third party, such as a consulting company or an outplacement agency, then the employee's permission needs to be sought in advance. The employee also has the right to ensure that the information being held is correct, and this will require companies to implement intranet systems so that the employee can only see their own record, and not that of others. For employees who have left the company this right will extend as long as their file is maintained, which also gives rise to a range of problems, such as the time for which a company should reasonably maintain that file.

The situation with regard to applications for positions, and for information about freelance staff, also needs careful consideration. It would seem that details about an applicant for a position in France, for example, cannot be transferred over an intranet to an office in the USA without the permission of the applicant. There are also issues with references provided by third parties, remembering that a person has the right of access to any personal information about themselves, and they also have the right to amend this information if it is incorrect. Since all intranets are assumed to be for the use of employees only, providing access to a third party needs careful consideration.

Another common situation is where a proposal is being prepared for an international client, and employee details are being accessed over an intranet to include in it. These details may include personal information, such as the employee's ability to work overseas for periods of time. If this information is exported from the EU to the USA it would seem that the employee will need to give their permission, yet at that stage the company may not wish to disclose to the employee that they are being considered for the project.

Data privacy is a major issue with search log analysis, especially in the EU. In reviewing intranet search logs, there could be searches for voluntary redundancy, sexual harassment or discrimination, or for the addresses of senior staff. These might be taken as an indication that the person carrying out these searches was planning to take redundancy, sue the organization for sexual harassment or discrimination, or send the addresses of senior managers to an animal rights activist group. The extent to which search logs might be construed to contain personal information has not yet been tested in the courts.[1]

Copyright

There will usually be a substantial amount of external content on an intranet, ranging from government circulars, legislation and regulations, to reports from external consultants and, increasingly, e-books. The extent to which these can be openly circulated to all employees will depend on the licence granted by the copyright holder. A similar situation will arise from the level of access provided to news clippings services and scientific databases. Copyright is a very complex subject and, again, legal advice is essential before any such content is added to the intranet.

Resource

1 http://ec.europa.eu/justice/policies/privacy/index_en.htm.

13
Enhancing the user experience

Introduction

Web usability has developed substantially over the last few years, thanks to the visionary work of Jakob Nielsen and Jared Spool in particular, but also as a result of the realization on the part of web managers that paying attention to web usability has a substantial benefit for the organization. The objective, as summed up so elegantly in the book of the same title by Steve Mulder, is 'don't make me think'. In general, good website design has reached such a level that, as users, we can immediately recognize and avoid a website in which the concept of usability has clearly not been considered by the web team. The range of resources on web usability is very wide, including a US government-supported website on the subject.

However, a search on www.usability.gov for 'intranet' reveals just seven references to intranets on the entire site, and several of these have little to do with usability testing. That is not to say that the principles of usable website design do not apply to intranets. Intranets present a very significant challenge because of the range of tasks that they typically support. Websites are highly focused on a relatively small number of tasks, most of which are likely to be the provision of information that will ensure that the visitor generates revenue for the website owner, either directly or indirectly.

In theory, intranet managers are in an enviable position because they have a fixed number of users and know their names, roles, locations and much else, information that is not available to a web manager. This advantage will be offset by the need to optimize a substantially wider and probably ill-defined set of tasks, and often a total lack of support for user-centric design and usability testing on the part of the organization. Lack of investment in usability testing is usually justified on the basis that the organization has invested in a search engine, and so if staff cannot find what they are looking for, then they can use the search engine.

The key elements of good usability are:

Ease of learning – How fast can a user who has never seen the user interface before learn it sufficiently well to accomplish basic tasks?

Efficiency of use – Once an experienced user has learned to use the system, how fast can he or she accomplish tasks?

Memorability – If a user has used the system before, can he or she remember enough to use it effectively the next time, or does the user have to start over again learning everything?

Error frequency and severity – How often do users make errors while using the system, how serious are these errors, and how do they recover from these errors?

Subjective satisfaction – How much does the user like using the system?

A related issue is accessibility, which is sometimes confused with usability but is more correctly defined as the extent to which the intranet can be used by employees with visual and other handicaps.

Usability testing is essential

There are many resources on the principles of usability testing, so the topic will not be covered in detail here. As far as good governance is concerned, the time and resources for usability testing need to be planned for. What is often not appreciated is that usability testing is not a one-off task to be performed when an intranet is first designed, or as part of a major redesign. An intranet is an ecosystem, and one small change in navigation or page management can have a substantial impact on the effective use of the intranet.

In one multinational company, lack of space on the home page meant that the link to the in-house travel service, operated by American Express (Amex), was removed. The travel department continued to exist, but it required a journey through four levels of navigation to reach the link to the travel site. Because no one had previously had to take this route staff resorted to using the search engine. In one month there were 817 searches on the word 'travel', 440 on 'Amex' and 374 on 'American Express'. Each one of these searches resulted in around 1000 hits, mainly because of innumerable memos highlighting the need to use the American Express Travel Services to book flights and hotels.

Three lessons can be learned from these results. First, about 1600 searches were being performed each month to find the travel site. Second, lack of resources in the search team meant that 'Amex' and 'American Express' generated a different number of results even though they refer to the same organization. Third, a significant amount of time was being wasted looking for the travel site because the relevance settings resulted in the travel site never appearing higher than 40th in the results list, whichever of the three search terms was used. The company was one in which international travel was very important, and yet a small change in the home page resulted not only in a great deal of time being wasted, but also in much frustration and annoyance that a key search was now so difficult to perform.

Usability testing has to be an ongoing process that

- takes account of users' feedback on how the intranet should be best organized for them to take full advantage of it

- ensures that, from the moment a new set of pages or a new application is introduced, at most only a few refinements will be needed to enable tasks to be accomplished as intuitively as possible.

The time to start usability testing on a proposed enhancement is not just before, or even just after, it is released. The process should start at the very beginning, using paper prototypes, then perhaps HTML wireframes that mimic the interactivity of that section of the site, followed by real-time user testing on a development server. This, of course, assumes that the organization has invested in a development/test server and is not forced to carry out the tests on a 'hidden' part of the live site that is probably already being crawled by the search engine and generating spurious results.

Time and time again

The view is often taken that no time is available for usability testing. There are two dimensions to the time requirement. One is the time taken to devise and perform the tests; the second is the time needed to review the results of the tests, make any necessary changes, and then perform a smaller set of acceptance tests to ensure that the changes do indeed work as required.

All this time, which can be considerable, needs to be balanced against the amount of time that can be wasted through users not being able to find the information they need. Just to take the example cited above, if 1600 users a month need an extra two minutes find the travel site, that amounts to around 53 hours wasted each month. A substantial amount of usability research could be conducted in the same amount of time.

The impact of poor usability should be measured not just in terms of lost productivity. If the information that is needed to make a decision cannot be found, will the best decision be taken? That is the challenge to throw into the governance mix, and it should not be ignored.

Accessibility

In the workplace there are many regulations about the way in which employees with visual and other handicaps should be supported. Under terms of the UN Convention on the Rights of Persons with Disabilities, which has been signed by the EU, persons with disabilities include those who have long-term physical, mental, intellectual or sensory impairments which, in their interaction with various barriers, may hinder their full and effective participation in society on an equal basis with others. The European Commission explicitly states in *The EU Internet Handbook*[1] that a web user (under the terms of the legislation) is 'the person who views the content of the website. In the case of an Intranet, it would be limited to those people belonging to the organization that owns the Intranet.'

So this legislation applies to the workplace as much as it does to access to publicly accessible web resources. However, little attention seems to have been paid to intranet-related issues, which in the UK fall under Part 2 of the Disability Discrimination Act (DDA) (there is similar legislation in all EU member states).

Section 4 of the DDA states: 'It is unlawful for an employer to discriminate against a disabled person whom he employs . . . in the opportunities which he affords him for . . . training . . . or [by] subjecting him to any other detriment.'

Section 5 of the DDA states: 'an employer discriminates against a disabled person if . . . for a reason which relates to the disabled person's disability, he treats him less favourably than he treats or would treat others to whom that reason does not or would not apply; and . . . he cannot show that the treatment in question is justified.'

Section 6 of the DDA states that where 'any arrangements made by or on behalf of an employer . . . place the disabled person concerned at a substantial disadvantage in comparison with persons who are not disabled, it is the duty of the employer to take such steps as it is reasonable, in all the circumstances of the case, for him to have to take in order to prevent the arrangements or feature having that effect.'

Because intranets provide basic information that helps staff to perform their normal duties, such as forms for holiday requests or appraisals, corporate policies and so on, a disabled person in the UK (as defined by the DDA) who was unable to access this information on a workplace intranet could argue that he was subject to a 'detriment' in terms of section 4; being treated 'less favourably' in terms of section 5;

and being put at a 'substantial disadvantage' in terms of section 6.

The importance of conforming to EU legislation caught Microsoft unaware when it launched MOSS07 and a patch to overcome the problems (associated with the underlying code on a SharePoint page) had to be rushed out. The situation seems to have been resolved to a significant extent in SharePoint 2010. It is important for intranet managers to ensure that the intranet is compliant with disability legislation.

Resources

1   The European Union has produced *The EU Internet Handbook*,
     http://ec.europa.eu/ipg/index_en.htm.

The following resources all cover the general subject of usability:

- Most of the many books on usability do not specifically cover the usability of intranets, although the basic principles are similar. Steve Mulder has written a very practical book on usability testing which takes into account current thinking about how to conduct usability tests: Mulder, S. (2009) *Rocket Surgery Made Easy: the do-it-yourself guide to finding and fixing usability problems*, Berkeley, CA: New Riders. This follows his previous bestselling book: Mulder, S. (2006) *Don't Make Me Think!: a common sense approach to web usability*, 2nd edn, Berkeley, CA: New Riders.
- A series of reports from the Nielsen Norman Group set out the basic principles of intranet usability: www.nngroup.com/reports/intranet/guidelines/.
- The US Government sponsors a very comprehensive website on all aspects of usability: www.usability.gov.
- Practical advice on web accessibility issues can be found in: Craven, J. (ed.) (2008) *Web Accessibility: practical advice for the library and information professional*, London: Facet Publishing.
- The Web Accessibility Initiative website is the definitive source of resources on accessibility compliance, which covers not only intranet users but also content contributors, whether working through a content management system or through social media applications: www.w3.org/WAI/.

14
Marketing the intranet

Introduction

One model of the way in which users adopt new technologies is the Gartner Technology Hype Cycle, illustrated in Figure 14.1. This model works well for intranets. The project begins from a technology trigger, such as the inability of the CMS to support user requirements, or the enterprise adoption of Microsoft SharePoint. Work begins on implementing the new technology platform and, especially among the senior management team, there are expectations that the new intranet will soon make a significant impact on business performance.

The reality is almost always that the technology enhancements tend to make life easier for content contributors and for the staff administering the intranet, but the impact on user experience is either quite small ('So why did we change the CMS?') or so major that users find they cannot

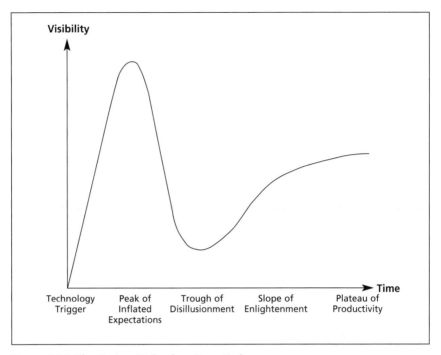

Figure 14.1 The Gartner Technology Hype Cycle

locate the information they need ('So why did we change the CMS?').
The Trough of Disillusionment has been reached. Gradually, users and
the intranet team find that there are some benefits from the technology
change, but that it takes time to reach, let alone exceed, Plateau of
Productivity of the previous system.

The intranet strategy needs to include a marketing strategy, the aim
of which is to deflate unrealistic expectations, not allow any significant
disillusionment to go unaddressed, and enlighten users regarding the
value and impact of the intranet. Other enterprise applications do not
need such a strategy because the people using them have no alternative
– the application is embedded in their daily work (such as Accounts or
HR) for compliance and audit reasons. This is rarely the case with the
intranet. Another difference between the intranet and, for example, the
HR system is that the value of the intranet to two people sitting next to
each other could be significantly different. One may be a long-term

employee who has spent much of their career in the organization in a variety of positions. The other may have just joined the organization and have a similar skill background, but gained in other industries. Each will take a very different view of the intranet.

Of course it is not possible to enhance the value and impact of an intranet until some are metrics in place (see Chapter 15) that enable the current situation to be determined – and the extent of a marketing campaign success to be measured.

Intranet brand identity

The first step is to decide on a brand identity for the intranet. A good starting point for a discussion on brand identity is the product attributes from Microsoft Product Reaction Cards. The brand identity for the intranet of a major law firm could well be substantially different from that for a charity that supports people working with single parents. The website of an organization will (or should) also have a strong brand identity, but it might not be appropriate to an intranet application. A police force website would probably have crime reduction as its core brand value, and although that would also be a core strategic objective for the force's intranet, the intranet's brand identity might be about working more closely together, or gaining operational effectiveness.

One of the best published accounts of the development of a brand identity can be found on the website of Step Two Designs.[1] It is a detailed description of the reasons why the City of Casey adopted a fairly light-hearted approach to an intranet called Boris. The viewpoint of Website Co-ordinator Michael Cleland is as follows:

> Simply put, our staff remember Boris. It's not just a system. The brand
> awareness of Boris is very high but, importantly, it's backed up by the fact
> that staff find it extremely easy to use and it has information that they need
> to help them in their jobs. The statistics back this up – staff use it regularly
> for everything from the staff directory, to payroll, news, bBay (our self-serve
> eBay-style trading post), HR, leave and more.

People simply refer to Boris as Boris. Just recently, someone said to me they were talking to someone outside our organization and said proudly, 'Oh, we don't have Lotus Notes, we've got Boris!'

There's a sense of ownership with Boris – he's not mine (although I do get called Boris's daddy) but he belongs to all of us. People just tell me, 'Boris is great!' They love the staff directory with the desk locator mapping and our easy-to-use trading post, bBay. New staff especially love him and tell me how much better he is than intranets at their previous employers.

If Boris was just 'CaseyNet' or some other boring name, it just wouldn't be the same.

As Step Two Designs comments:

The City of Casey's Boris branding exercise stands as a great example of how to kick-start your intranet's existence and maintain its visibility in the long term.

While the character itself may not be to everyone's taste, or a fit for every organization's culture, the underlying concept is strong and there's no doubting the character has personality and his presence catches the attention of employees.

Furthermore, the brand is supported by useful applications including the award-winning Staff Locator (a Gold Award winner in the 2007 Intranet Innovation Awards), the staff directory, the trading post (bBay) and more.

If Boris was simply a brand for a site that was of little use then users would soon lose interest – no matter how fresh the graphics. But because of the usefulness of the site, Boris serves as the glue, providing cohesion and a virtual buddy who will help.

One of the greatest challenges in developing an intranet brand is the extent to which it should be a 'fun' application. The evidence is that some element of 'fun' can be useful in an application that will be on everyone's desktop every day. Whether the fun element is some form of employee survey or a video of the organization's last charity fun run has to be decided on a case-by-case basis. It is a mistake to make an a priori decision that the intranet is a business application and that there should be no 'fun' element. Only if the organization also bans humour from business meetings might it be a justifiable approach!

Giving the intranet a name

The one certainty about giving an intranet a name is that changing its name just so as to revitalize an intranet that has otherwise fallen into disuse is not going to make any difference. Almost any name is preferable to 'The Intranet'. Organizations invest significant amounts of money in developing a name for the monthly staff newsletter, but fail to see the importance of giving the intranet the same treatment.

The intranet's name needs to be aligned with the culture of the organization and the brand identity of the application. The City of Casey finds that 'Boris' works well, but it might not be such a good idea for a law firm, and clearly there is also a risk that someone with the same name will join the organization – possibly at a senior level. There is something to be said for not creating a persona for the intranet, but for taking a more inanimate approach to naming it.

Many organizations run a competition for naming the intranet. Although it can generate a high level of interest, sometimes it also results in a name that is the best of a very poor set of contributions. Attention may need to be paid to cultural issues, and to how well the name works in several different languages. Some years ago Rolls-Royce planned to name a new model of car the Rolls-Royce Mist, until someone realized that in German the word 'Mist' means manure.

Giving the intranet team visibility

All too often the most invisible element of the intranet is the identity of the team working on it. Although there is a feedback form for sending messages to 'the intranet manager' or a similar entity, there is no easy way to find out anything about the intranet team or about the work it does to support the intranet. Because the value and impact of an intranet will be different for each user, it is essential for users to feel that they can have one-on-one contact with someone from the intranet team.

If the intranet team members are working on a part-time basis they may feel concerned about receiving too much feedback from users. That is putting the cart before the horse. If the feedback is positive, it can be used to create a business case for more staff. If the feedback is critical, especially in the areas of trust and the intranet's impact on users, the organization needs to take note of such comments.

The intranet team is in a position to set standards. This could be in the form of a set of pages describing the intranet, or a blog of user alerts to what is coming up in the near future. A well written blog will then set a standard for other bloggers.

Cups and mats and fancy hats

The imagination can run riot when it comes to promotional items such as cups and mugs proudly displaying the name of the intranet. These incentive (if not inventive) products can have a role in the early stages of a major launch or relaunch, but probably for only a very limited time. The challenge lies not in making users aware of the new name, but in getting them to use the intranet in a way that will benefit them and the organization.

This is the time to consider the marketing message:

- We've expanded the staff directory and this will make it much easier to find staff with specific expertise.
- People can now complete their expenses forms and travel requisitions online.
- We have a much improved Jobs Vacant section that takes people right through from filing their CV to arranging a time for an interview.
- We've created a new list of projects so that the engineers writing the proposals can easily find examples of previous proposals.
- The Chief Executive is going to start a personal blog.

Each of these could be promoted in different ways. The challenge is not to reach the stage that users feel you are shouting at them or notice that the 'new' posters have been up on the staff restaurant notice board for seven months.[2]

With all these physical reminders of the intranet, it is important to consider whether every office, or every country, will be able to distribute them. As with naming the intranet, cultural attitudes to different items may vary. What works for a corporate headquarters in Ohio might not work for a small but important project office in Sri Lanka.

Nothing succeeds like success

It is one thing to promote a new staff directory, and another to get people to use it in the best possible way. Intranet processes can be complicated and it is important to get beyond the functionality and show how someone in the organization has made themselves into a hero by using the intranet. No matter how committed people are to the organization that employs them, personal visibility and praise are very important. If John has won a major contract because of the way he tracked down company experts by using the staff directory and looking through blogs, then a story about his success should be on the intranet, and also in the staff magazine. There might also be a case for e-mailing (as a link) to people doing similar tasks in other offices and countries. A popular approach with an intranet relaunch is to set up a quiz or scavenger hunt on the intranet. GE used this approach and offered an Amazon token as the prize.

This is something that Amazon and other retailers discovered a few years ago – that there is nothing like a review to sell a book, a CD or a holiday. People are not concerned that they know nothing about the reviewer. The very fact that there is a review, or a success story, will make them want to have or do the same thing.

Finding the stories can take time, and a lot of walking around, but it will be much easier if the intranet team is not only visible but also signals that this is the type of story it is looking for. Every member of the intranet management team should be on the look-out for such stories, perhaps identifying them through regular staff meetings.

Extranet marketing

Undoubtedly, adding functionality that enables suppliers and or customers to access sections of the intranet will be a significant investment for an organization, yet often little is done to promote the application to external stakeholders. Because of the way in which access permissions are granted, almost certainly detailed information will be available as to which stakeholder has visited which pages.

Increasing the value and impact of an extranet requires a two-pronged approach. First, employees with customer contact need to be kept fully informed about the functionality and content of the extranet and to be aware of when their customers last used it. Second, there should be intranet manager-to-intranet manager communication to ensure that relevant pages in the stakeholder intranet are linked into the extranet. There have been cases of an organization's intranet manager having no idea of the existence of extranet facilities for their users.

Resources

1   Step Two Designs' account of the branding of 'Boris' can be found at:
    www.steptwo.com.au/papers/kmc_cityofcasey/index.html.
2   Good examples of intranet marketing can be found in the reports of the
    Intranet Innovation Awards, published by Step Two Designs:
    www.steptwo.com.au/iia
    and in the annual reports *Intranet Design Annual* from the Nielsen Norman
    Group:
    www.nngroup.com/reports/intranet/design/.

15
Measuring user satisfaction

Introduction

Intranet managers seem to be on an almost perpetual quest to find ways to justify not only investment in the intranet, but almost the very existence of the application. This is not the case for other enterprise systems. The finance director is not asked to justify the accounting system, nor the personnel director the HR system. The reasons for this have already been discussed. It is therefore important for the governance strategy to present a range of ways in which the value and impact of the intranet can be assessed. This chapter sets out a wide range of options for consideration.

All too often procedures for measuring value and impact are implemented only when a need for investment is seen on the horizon. The result will be that metrics dating back only a few months are available making it difficult for all concerned to work out whether the peaks and troughs are real, an artefact of poor server performance, or indicate the start-up of a major project that required intensive research.

The challenge is to develop a balance between absolute metrics (number of documents downloaded) and relative metrics (percentage increase of documents), and between quantitative metrics (number of users per working day) and qualitative metrics (level of trust in intranet content). This chapter sets out a range of approaches, but to use all of them is unrealistic. The choice of approach must take into account available resources and the way in which the organization typically makes investment decisions.

Website logs

In the website business, logs of clicks and downloads are essential for optimizing the site and justifying enhancements to the technology and the content. Data on page hits alone can be quite useful, but the paths that people take through the site before taking an action to buy or download also provide very valuable information. It is also widely recognized that visitors to a website often arrive via a search site, such as Google; knowing which page they land on when arriving is important in developing effective routes through the site.

Many years ago, at a KMWorld/Intranets conference in California, a speaker suggested that in the intranet world HITS was an acronym for How Idiots Track Success of an intranet. This is perhaps an extreme view, but not far from the truth. A few years ago a company was heavily involved in developing its business interests in China. A search on 'China business' produced a hit in the first page of results for the Royal Maroc Airlines website, where one page carried the information that china crockery was used in the airline's business class. A check on the website logs showed that this page was among the top ten pages viewed, because people clicked on it, in amazement that it had been cached into the intranet.

One of the problems with website statistics for an intranet is managing the number of pages that are clicked on in the course of a day. For a website perhaps only a dozen pages can give a good indication of whether a marketing campaign is working. For an intranet with in excess of 500,000 pages, which ones will provide the best reflection of value? It is probably impossible to say.

Using website logs as a focused diagnostic tool can be very valuable, especially when changes are being made to the intranet and their impact on users needs to be assessed. Using them to track paths through an intranet is challenging, and takes up a lot of time. That is the issue with any application where quantitative statistical information needs to be turned into actionable intelligence; the intranet teams need to balance the effort against the benefit.

Search logs

In general, search logs are more valuable. Most vendors will provide search logs, but sometimes they can be quite basic in the level of detail. In general, it is best to export the data into a graphics analysis package, and vendors should be asked not only which packages they know work well with their product, but also to include some typical logs from a customer installation in their selection presentation. The normal periodicities are the last seven days, the last 30 days and the last year, but the frequency needs to be under the control of the customer and not hard coded into the application.

In large organizations probably thousands of searches are performed each day, and the volume of data generated can be overwhelming. Too many organizations seem to take the view that they will look at the logs when time permits, and so no consistent base line is developed – perhaps on a monthly basis – that will enable trends and exceptions to be identified with confidence.

The most useful log reports are described here. For the purposes of this chapter the number of searches has been arbitrarily set at 50, but in practice the number will need to be determined on an ad hoc basis as the scale and value of the log files become apparent.

Number of searches per hour/day

As an enterprise total, this metric has little merit other than to impress the CEO. At a subsidiary or country level, and on an application basis, it can indicate how well training courses seem to be working, or countries that may be having major problems in using the application – which could be caused by network access problems rather than a lack of demand. As with all logs, it is the deviations from normal that are important.

Top 50 searches by search terms/query

The purpose is to see which searches are the most popular – and some of them could well be symptomatic of poor information architecture on the intranet(s). Even if the enterprise search is working across multiple repositories, it is likely that the intranet will be the starting point for the majority of searches. In one company it became apparent that most of the top search terms resulted from searches for applications such as teleconference numbers or the travel booking application. Using a search application to find this type of information will always return many hits and the user then has to work out which one is the application and which are the dozen or so internal memos that have been circulated over the last few years about the need to use the travel application.

Top 50 searches leading to no or very few results being presented

This log will show where there may be gaps in content, or where a search query is being typed incorrectly and the internal directories are not suggesting an appropriate alternative. A user may have chosen the wrong collection or used the wrong acronym for an internal project or product. These really need to be looked at as a matter of urgency, because the lack of results will worry the searcher and mean that they will then phone someone, hoping that the lack of a response is just due to their inexperience.

Top 50 searches leading to no document being selected or page opened

This is a situation that needs careful scrutiny. Users are being presented with a list of results, but either they are very wide of the mark or the user has realized that they need to go to a specific section of the intranet or another application to find the required information.

Top 50 most requested documents

Some of these may need to be promoted to Best Bets. A review of the list may also show that users are viewing documents that are in fact out of date or not a best match. These insights can only come from search team members who know the significance of these failures and can devote time to finding out why users have selected the documents.

Top 50 searches where more than three pages of hits were presented

This analysis should give some indication of where the relevance ranking needs attention, especially if the documents being retrieved were some way down the list of hits. If searches are resulting in several hundred or more hits, users are likely to give up and try something else. This again could indicate a strong case for looking at the information architecture of the site.

Help desk query analysis

Many departments in the organization will have a help desk, even if it does not have that name. In the case of IT there will certainly be a help desk, and often HR departments and libraries will have one. Dealing with queries takes a lot of staff time and can be frustrating when the enquiry can easily be satisfied by looking at the intranet. An organization had a very good A–Z list of forms, among which was the form that department managers had to complete to initiate recruitment of new members of staff. Was it under R for Recruitment? No. That would be too easy. It was under B, listed as the Bias-Free Recruitment Form, having recently been amended to take account of UK racial discrimination legislation. The document's title was changed, resulting in a useful reduction in the number of calls to the HR help desk.

Working with the people staffing these desks will almost always indicate where the intranet can relieve the pressure – a time metric that can quite easily be converted into a cost-saving in terms of staff time, as well as enabling staff to get on with important business without having to break off and deal with queries.

Employee climate surveys

These have a variety of names within organizations and tend to be annual surveys of employees' attitudes to their working environment and the culture of the organization. Since they are often managed by the internal communications department they can be biased towards assessing the effectiveness of communications channels. Just occasionally, especially if the internal communications department has ownership of the intranet, there will be a question such as:

- How valuable is the intranet to you?

Few people are going to give a straight answer, if only because it is such a general question. The intranet deserves more than just this one question, given the specific nature of the following replies:

- Compared to last year, I rely more on the intranet to provide the information I need to make fast and effective decisions.

- It would be more difficult for me to meet my personal objectives if I felt I could not trust the quality of the information on the intranet.
- I am confident that when I find information on the intranet I trust it to be the best and most current information available in the organization.

Using a scaled response format, each of these statements can be ranked either numerically or by a range of options from 'Totally agree' to 'Totally disagree'.

In some multinational organizations there are national surveys. Taking a consistent approach to surveys is very valuable, as this means that comparative information can be developed about, for example, the value of the local intranet compared with information provided in a global home page or by global departments.

As with all such surveys, the annual trends are more important than spot data, which is why care should be taken to ensure that a slight change in the questions will not devalue the trend information or create a gap in information for a crucial year.

User surveys

The wide availability of web survey applications makes it easy for intranet managers to develop user surveys without involving IT developers. However, the ease with which a survey can be carried out can mean little time is spent in developing the questionnaire, and no time at all is spent on piloting it. Running a pilot is essential, as it is easy to wrongly assume that everyone in the organization understands exactly what a question means.

Questions such as:

- How often do you use the intranet?

will be of no value unless there is awareness of context relating to the user and the purpose for which the intranet is being used. A survey is usually of greatest value when it is carefully targeted at a user group, and this is where the work on personas and tasks (see Chapter 2) can have significant benefits. For example, a survey targeted at new employees will help to find out whether, compared with last year, their early confusion about the workings of the organization has been reduced as a result of changes to some of the sections of the intranet. New employees will be pleased to feel that their opinions are valued. They will probably have more recent experience of other intranets than anyone else in the organization, so another useful question to ask would be whether they had used other intranet applications in their previous jobs that they would find useful.

One of the most common scaled response-format questions in survey design today is the Likert scale. It was developed by the American educator and organizational psychologist Rensis Likert in 1932, in an attempt to improve the levels of measurement in social research by using standardized response categories in survey questionnaires.

A commonly used five-point Likert-scale format for measuring satisfaction is:

1 Very satisfied
2 Satisfied
3 Neither satisfied nor dissatisfied
4 Dissatisfied
5 Very dissatisfied

Another that can be found in some satisfaction surveys is the six-point Likert scale, which reads:

1 Extremely satisfied
2 Very satisfied
3 Somewhat satisfied
4 Somewhat dissatisfied
5 Very dissatisfied
6 Extremely dissatisfied

There is much debate in the survey business about which is the 'best' approach and it is well worth doing an internet search on 'Likert scales' and reading some of the wealth of articles for one side or the other. There is no consensus on which is best, but at least you will gather some evidence to argue the case for whichever one you select.

Language is a crucial factor in achieving a good survey response, and the Likert scale above is a good example. The nuances of the English language are often only apparent to people who have English as a second or even a third language; even the use of a word like 'somewhat' is fraught with difficulty. In a multiple-language environment it is recommended to give careful consideration to the need for multiple language surveys, even if English is the default language, or at least to test the survey in countries where there could be some difficulties with English comprehension.

Users should be able to complete a survey in the time it takes to drink a cup of coffee – even better, in the time it takes to drink a cup of water. That is why a pilot is so important. The initial questions need to be capable of being answered in a few seconds. A scale that indicates how much of the survey remains to be completed is a good idea.

Real value can come from including a free-text box at the end of the survey. One idea that works well is to ask respondents to give examples, in no more than 100 words, both of where the intranet has been of significant help and of where it has failed to deliver. The good news can go direct to the CEO, and the bad news will often show that the problems arise from poor-quality content, not being able to find content, inability to be sure that the content is the most current and dependable, and the respondent having an inflated expectation of what the intranet can actually deliver.

Maintaining respondent confidentiality is very important, but some basic information about department, role and length of time with the organization will be very useful. At the end of the survey it can be helpful to ask if the respondent would be willing to talk in more detail to the intranet team about a particular issue.

All the evidence points to the fact that surveys are more likely to be completed well if there is fast and open communication of the results, and if the intranet team also communicate about the actions that they plan to take – even if all they can give is an honest response that changes cannot be made until a new WCMS is installed or another person can be recruited to the intranet team. Surveys take more time to devise, test, implement and analyse than most people without a market research background ever appreciate. A poorly conceived survey will be a total waste of even the minimal effort that is put into it.

Pop-up surveys

It is also possible to install survey software that is triggered by a specific URL. So, for example, when an employee clicks on the office location section two or three very specific questions can be asked. People can find this intrusive, so some basic guidelines need to be followed:

- Alert users to the fact that the survey is being undertaken.
- Enable people to click off the box, or give them a chance to complete the survey later.
- Run the survey for only a short period of time.
- Feed back the results as quickly as possible.

Feedback forms

Every intranet should have a feedback form, with a link on the main tool bar that is visible on every page. The key success factor in obtaining feedback from users is the contract between the user and the intranet team. It should be clearly stated that feedback will be acknowledged within one working day (or whatever is reasonable); and the response should contain an indication of what action will be taken. This might range from checking out an item of incorrect content, and removing it if appropriate, to raising the subject at the next meeting of the intranet operations group. This immediate response conveys to the user that their comment is valued.

However, the really important response might be the outcome of a meeting of the intranet operations group, and this is often overlooked. It might be worth investing in a help desk ticketing system, hosted either on the intranet server or externally. These systems allow tracking of partially resolved comments and parameters such as the average time to resolution. These applications are not only of value in large organizations; they can be just as valuable, possibly even more so, in situations where the intranet manager is doing several other jobs and could easily lose track of follow-up action on a comment or suggestion.

It can be helpful to publish the outcomes of feedback from users, as this is a clear demonstration that the intranet team is not only listening but also acting on the comments it receives.

Attendance at meetings

Intranet managers can sometimes appear to be invisible and anonymous. One way to ensure that this does not happen is for him or her to sit in on meetings, or lurk on collaboration sites. Attending the quarterly meeting of the marketing department and having the intranet on the agenda does require a degree of self-confidence on the part of the intranet manager, but there can be great value in sitting in and listening to real-world problems.

Some years ago Nortel, a Canadian telecommunications company, took the step of ensuring that the PCs in all its meeting rooms were live at the home page of the intranet. Nowadays people tend to bring their own laptops to meetings. But there should at least be a note in every meeting room reminding attendees that the intranet is accessible, should any issues arise during the meeting that could be solved there and then through using it.

Persona advocate interviews

The value of a persona advocate has been described in Chapter 2. Once the intranet design issues have been sorted out the value of the advocate continues. An interview, either in person or by telephone, will make the advocate feel that their efforts in the development stage have been of value and will enable both parties to reflect on the outcomes of the persona work. Organizations change very rapidly, something that is likely to be the case for the foreseeable future. The persona advocate is in a very good position to assess how the changes might usefully be reflected in the intranet.

Outside of an occasional meeting, the persona advocate should also be reassured that they have a direct line into the intranet team at any time if they sense either that there is good news to report (and publicize!) or there are some actual or potential problems.

It may well be worth holding a yearly meeting of all the persona advocates, especially if one wishes to step down and wants to bring a colleague along so as to understand what might be involved. Of course, this is more difficult in a multinational organization, but the principle is an important one to keep under review. Intranet managers need friends within the organization!

Changes in the risk profile

The value of taking a risk management approach to developing a business case has been set out in Chapter 3, but as with the persona advocates there is ongoing value in maintaining the approach. A meeting with the risk manager might well identify where a risk has been downgraded because of the impact of the intranet, or indicate an emerging risk that the intranet could have an important role in ameliorating. There will not be many instances of either situation, but when they do arise their value for the confidence of the intranet team can be tremendous.

Search for 'intranet'

It can be interesting and revealing to carry out a search for 'intranet' on the intranet. The results should, of course, list out all the pages of content that mention the word 'intranet'. These can be useful to work through so as to ensure that references to the intranet remain clear and current. But where there is an environment of active collaboration the search may well reveal comments about where staff cannot find content on the intranet, advice on how to find content, and general comments about the value (or otherwise) of the application.

Workplace penetration

Often intranet managers do not know how many direct and indirect intranet users there are. Direct users are those who have access through a desktop, and indirect users can be front-line staff who may use a walk-up terminal, have some sections of the intranet available on their shop sales tills (a practice used by Boots the chemists in the UK), or depend for their daily list of priorities on information that their manager has obtained from the intranet. The intranet is a 'high touch' application, and knowing that 75% of all employees have desktop access, 13% access it through a kiosk and 12% have a summary via a podcast (the Swiss Post Office) can make negotiating resources and investment a little easier.

Intranet associates

In many departments there may be one or more members of staff who either are significant content contributors or make heavy use of the intranet. They could be appointed as intranet associates and have a small 'certificate' to place on their desk. These people can act as the eyes and ears of colleagues to identify problems and requirements that need to be addressed.

Intranet blog

An intranet blog with an option for readers to add comments can be a very good way of capturing suggestions. It could also be an effective channel for informing employees about issues that have been raised through other routes. Seeing some initial suggestions will also catalyse others – no one wants to be the first to make a suggestion!

E-mail

How easy is it for any member of staff to find the members of the intranet team and send an e-mail with a suggestion or a comment? Sometimes the very simple ways are also the most effective.

Benchmarking

Over the last few years intranet benchmarking has gained a high visibility and credibility through the work of the Intranet Benchmarking Forum. The benchmarking methodology developed by this organization has evolved over a number of years and through the experience gained from undertaking benchmarking projects for member organizations. The aim of all benchmarking methodologies is to define good practice, the problem being that good practice changes unpredictably. A good example is the extent to which social media applications are integrated into the intranet, where good practice is evolving quite quickly.

The Intranet Benchmarking Forum methodology[1] takes a small team of consultants several days to complete; it then presents the results to the member organization. Members find it very valuable in prioritizing actions to raise the standard of the organization's intranet. The methodology is kept under continual review and new elements are added from time to time. The Forum also supports a number of special interest groups.

There are other approaches to benchmarking. In 2006 Step Two Designs developed an Intranet Review Toolkit[2] which uses a heuristic approach to benchmarking. A typical heuristic would be 'Scrolling is minimised on the home page' and a score of 1 to 5 is given, depending on whether, for the intranet in question, the scroll is at least three pages (score 1) or a single page (score 5).

The toolkit covers:

- home page
- site structure and navigation
- search
- page layout and visual design
- intranet content
- news
- staff directory
- intranet-based applications
- intranet strategy and management.

Using the toolkit, the benchmark can be performed by the intranet manager and typically takes about three hours to work through. It is a very useful first-level diagnostic, but now needs updating to meet the emerging elements and uses of intranets, such as social media.

Another approach is offered by CIBA Solutions with its Worldwide Intranet Challenge.[3] A web-based survey enables users to give their opinions on how well the intranet meets their needs. It covers:

* completing work tasks
* quantity and quality of content
* ease of finding information
* employee interaction and engagement
* intranet change management
* look and feel
* performance and availability.

Finally, there are consultants around the world who specialize in intranet development consultancy and who will often start a project by benchmarking the current intranet.

There are three common issues with benchmarking that need to be taken into consideration when using any of these methodologies:

* Where will the benchmarking add value to the work that is already being carried out in monitoring and addressing user requirements?
* What approach will the intranet team take if the recommendations of the benchmark report seem to be at odds with the information available to the team from user research?
* How will senior managers react to seeing a comparative positioning of the intranet in relation to those in other organizations? Will they be stimulated to increase investment in the intranet, or be upset that the organization is somewhat behind other similar organizations and blame the intranet team?

There are two international competitions that the intranet team can enter as a way of obtaining an external assessment of the intranet. Each year the Nielsen Norman Group invites organizations to submit their intranets to be evaluated for the 10 Best Intranets Award.[4] There is also an annual Intranet Innovation Award competition sponsored by Step Two Designs.[5] In addition, there are some national competitions, such as those run in Russia, Denmark and Switzerland.

Using an intranet consultant

There are still very few intranet consultants – which is good for the consultants concerned, but not for companies seeking advice on their intranet operations. When selecting an intranet consultant there is one important point to consider, and that is whether they are independent of any software provider, so that there will be no danger of receiving biased recommendations.

There are many consultants working for Microsoft and IBM systems partners who have a lot of experience in intranets, but they will have an understandable loyalty to the technology platform of their direct or indirect employer. In some situations this can be beneficial, as they may be able to identify ways in which the current implementation of, say, Microsoft SharePoint is not optimal for the organization.

If an external consultant is needed to undertake research on user requirements and provide a synthesis of the outcomes, any link to an IT supplier is unlikely to be an issue.

Resources

1   Details of the membership benefits offered by the Intranet Benchmarking Forum can be found at:
    www.ibforum.com.
2   The Intranet Review Toolkit can be downloaded from:
    www.steptwo.com.au/products/irtoolkit.
3   Information about the World Wide Intranet Benchmarking Challenge can be found at:
    www.cibasolutions.com.au/.
4   www.nngroup.com.
5   www.steptwo.com.au/iia

Part 4
Governance and strategy

16
Creating the governance framework

Introduction

Any decision we make, in business or in our life outside the office, will have a risk and a benefit. The better the quality of information we have available to us, the more likely that the trade-off between risk and benefit will be to our advantage. Governance, a very over-used buzz-word of the past decade, is about putting in place procedures to ensure that the people making decisions:

• have the authority to do so
• have all the relevant information before making the decision
• are aware of the *impact* of the decision on all who may be affected
• keep a clear record of the decision.

Governance is therefore concerned with:

- defining the decisions that need to be made in order to achieve an objective
- the roles and responsibilities of individuals who will make or influence those decisions
- the organizational structure of the business and how the individuals involved in making or influencing decisions can share their views
- establishing policies and procedures that support or constrain the process of decision making
- providing information that establishes the current state of affairs, so that the impact of any decision can be assessed.

Whenever two or three intranet managers gather together, the subject of the conversation soon turns to governance issues, and in particular the 'governance structure' of each other's intranet.[1] When intranets fail to meet business and user requirements it is rarely due to a problem with the technology or to incompetence on the part of the intranet manager. They fail because decisions need to be made but no one seems to have either the authority to make them or the vision to understand the impact that either the optimum decision or no decision at all will have on the organization. When I undertake intranet consulting assignments one of my conditions of engagement is that I will have access to either the CEO (if the organization is reasonably small) or a member of the senior management team. My reason is not only to get a top-down view of what they see as the objectives for the intranet, but also to find out who they think is responsible for making decisions about how to achieve these objectives. I have regularly come across situations where senior managers are not sure who 'owns' the intranet.

It is not just a question of operational ownership. There will come times when the decision making is beyond the role of the nominal owner. At that point it generally becomes clear that no process is in place for escalating the matter to a more senior level – something that is especially needed when two departments 'own' the intranet and neither is willing to increase their funding to meet increasing user demands.

The problems and challenges are summed up in Figure 16.1.

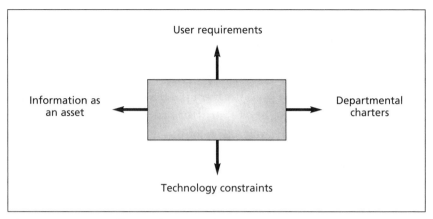

Figure 16.1 Factors affecting decision making

We will look at each of these elements in turn.

User requirements – Information is contextual to the individual. Two people with the same experience and the same roles may well place a different value on any piece of information that is common to them. It is all about relevance, which is inherently personal. Intranet managers have an almost impossible task in trying to find generic solutions to individual requirements, which are often poorly expressed.

Departmental charters – Very few departments have a charter that extends to each employee, and the remit of those that do is often limited to a specific country or even a specific subsidiary. Because HR, IT and internal communications departments do have charters to support all employees it is often these departments that end up owning the intranet, whether or not they have the interest and commitment to do so.

Technology constraints – These constraints may be both technical and financial, with the result that the CMS used for the intranet cannot meet the requirements of users. In some cases the organization may have decreed that SharePoint is the corporate standard and the intranet has to be run on this platform.

Information as an asset – Most organizations still fail to realize that
information is an asset and needs to be managed in an
appropriate way. In such circumstances, ensuring that the
intranet can play an appropriate role in information provision will
always be a challenge.

Each of these four factors pulls the intranet in a particular direction, and
the challenge of any governance structure is to maintain an informed
balance such that the intranet can play the maximum possible role in
providing information for all employees.

However, there is one factor missing from the above, and that is the
reporting line and career development of the intranet team, which is
often very important. Indeed, the reporting relationship of the
intranet manager is often a deciding factor in the ownership of the
intranet. In many years of consulting on intranet strategy – in which
governance issues play such a major role – I have yet to hear a
discussion about governance that takes into account the career
interests of the intranet manager. The discussion always seems to
centre on departmental politics and how managing the intranet will
enable the department to have a larger budget without having to be
too explicit about how it will be spent.

Intranet ownership

The interests of the department(s) owning the intranet will shape the
objectives of the intranet. When the intranet is owned by the
communications department, then the focus will inevitably be on
organizational news and shaping the culture of the organization.

In general, ownership by the IT department tends to be fairly benign.
Intranets are just not technically interesting to IT departments, unless
SharePoint is the enterprise information platform of choice. In that case,
IT will usually make a strong case for owning the intranet, as a showcase
for the talents of the development team.

If the owners are not communications and/or IT, then HR will step up
as the owner. This department will see the benefit in implementing self-
service HR applications and using the intranet to reduce staff costs. HR

departments also have an interest in training and work practices, and often in organizational development.

What is notable about all three departments is that they are corporate departments with responsibilities to all employees, but with no direct responsibility to deliver to customers. That is certainly not to say that the organization could function without them; but none of these three departments is involved in developing new products, worrying about customer retention or working in teams with a range of external stakeholders to develop new business opportunities.

Is democracy the answer?

Many organizations seem to take the approach of ensuring that all potential stakeholders are represented on one or other of the committees set up to govern the intranet. This is usually an attempt to defuse any moves by individual departments or subsidiaries to go off and do their own thing, so it tends to be defensive in its approach and usually results in too much time being spent in trying to achieve a consensus. This is because the individual committees are usually too large for effective management, and departments will often send a substitute delegate to meetings – because, after all, it is only the intranet that is being discussed. If departments knew the reliance their staff placed on the intranet, they might take a different position!

However, all of these structures lose sight of the granularity of interests set out in the so-called RACI framework that is often used to develop governance models:

Responsible – the position responsible for seeing that the work is done (the 'doers')

Accountable – the position with responsibility and authority to approve/reject a task or action

Consulted – person(s) who has to be consulted about a task or action and who needs to provide an input and be 'kept in the loop' by two-way communication

Informed – person(s) who need to be informed about the task or action and is 'kept in the picture' by one-way communication.

All too often committees are set up without analysing the different roles that people play and the scope that they have, as members, to make decisions. Often they have no remit to make decisions on behalf of their department and have to go back and seek guidance, thus prolonging the decision-making process.

Follow the money

Intranet managers often complain that they need a decision on X but they and the various committees that have been set up are unsure where the decision-making responsibility resides. Decisions usually mean spending money, either directly or indirectly, and this is the core of the problem, because intranet budgets are invariably departmental budgets. The internal communications budget may well include a budget line for the salaries and associated costs of running the intranet on behalf of the entire organization. This usually works well at the outset. But when the department comes under pressure to reduce head count or spending its priority will be to make sure that its own house is in order and it has reduced spending by the required amount. Even if another department, say HR, is willing to allocate a budget to the intranet, the accounts department may have no cost code for the intranet that it can transfer from the one department to the other.

This issue of cost codes can make or break an intranet budget because the codes have a taxonomy all of their own that links into audit processes and both management and financial accounting. Arguably, a core area of knowledge for any intranet manager should be to understand the organization's accounting codes and cost centres. It can be the case that the manager concerned is willing to allocate budget but does not know how to make it all work. If the intranet manager is able to say that by using cost code 1345R everything will be taken care of, that can be a very effective way of making money appear in the right place for the right purpose.

When I start a project, as well as meeting the CEO I also ask to see someone from the finance department who can explain the cost codes and, in particular, departmental recharging polices for the intranet. It can then be very interesting to match the codes and recharges to the people responsible for authorizing expenditure against the cost code. That is the way organizations work, and knowing how they work in budget management terms is a key item of knowledge for any intranet manager.

Another challenge that has to be faced is that budgets are allocated on an annual basis – but the intranet goes on forever. A reduction in head count could have an impact for many years to come.

Building governance around decisions

There are some fundamental principles of intranet decision making that need to be incorporated into any governance structure:

- Each year different decisions will need to be made, both because of the growing maturity of the intranet and because the organizational climate will change.
- Decisions should only be made by people who have the remit to make them and ensure that they are carried through.
- Decisions almost always involve trade-offs between various options.
- The more direct the impact of a decision on organizational performance, the more quickly it will be made.
- A decision based on a consensus is not necessarily the best decision.
- A decision is only as good as the information it is based on and the experience of the decision maker.

What are the implications of these principles? The first is it needs to be recognized that even if the constitution of a committee does not change from year to year, the membership will almost certainly do so. Take the case of a typical intranet steering group. The challenge in 2011 could be to reduce the time between invitation to bid and delivery of the project proposal to the client, and at the same time to increase the number of successful bids by number, value and contribution. The intranet steering group may view this as a very good business case for enhancing the collaboration functionality available to bid managers.

In 2012 the company may decide that the best way to exploit its new financial strength is to acquire a company in Spain that provides a complementary range of services to a common customer base. Now the HR and internal communications departments will see the intranet as a core platform for realizing the synergies from the acquisition and integration. Intranet developments might include enhancing e-form platforms to enable expenses claims to be submitted in different currencies, or writing a new staff induction section in Spanish.

It can be very valuable to create a rolling three-year plan identifying decisions that need to be made for the continuing development of the intranet. Examples might include when to migrate to SharePoint 2010; replacement of the search engine; or implementing a facility for staff to comment on content. Each decision will have three elements:

> The decision we need to make is [. . .] so that we are able to [. . .], which will then ensure that the business requirement for [. . .] is met.

Once the decisions have been identified the next step is to decide who is best placed to make them. It may not be possible to bring the final decision makers on to the intranet steering group, even though this may be very desirable. But under no circumstances should there be anyone on the steering group who does not report directly to the ultimate decision maker – either the CIO or the CFO – nor should they have to report back to a committee in order to get a decision. Business needs move too quickly for one committee to have to refer to another and then report back to the initial body.

Most decisions in business are not simple to make. There will be trade-offs within the intranet itself and also between the intranet and other applications. Senior managers, in particular, are sceptical when presented with a specific recommendation and no options. If the intranet team presents, say, three options, each of which clearly states what the trade-offs might be, this will reassure them that the team has thought through the issues.

To give an example, a proposal might be to appoint two people to manage the new enterprise search application. While it might be easy to identify the benefits, in the current climate head count could be a problem. An option might be just to appoint one person in the first year and save a certain amount of money. The drawback of this option might be that if there is no well defined career path and the salary grade is quite low the organization might be vulnerable to the appointee leaving; and if the person did leave, the search logs might not be actioned for six months, even if the reports were run.

Reaching a decision

Because of the inherent complexity of an intranet, with multiple stakeholders and usually multiple objectives, examining the trade-offs between the options for development and enhancement can be complex and time consuming, and in the end there will often be a small group who feel that their own requirements have not been fully understood and evaluated.

A good group decision will have the following characteristics:

- It must be carried out.
- It must take into account both facts and opinions.
- Everyone involved should be clear about the consequences.
- It must take self-interest principles into consideration.
- It must be derived from input from those parties who will be affected by it.
- It must make sense to all participants.

There are a number of methodologies that can be used to encourage the participants to focus on the essential elements of a decision, such as decision matrices, force field analysis and T-charting. In the case of intranet governance, forced-pair analysis can be a way of getting all those involved to state their views on priorities explicitly, rather than by using body language.

Figure 16.2 shows four options for the next application to be developed. For each intersection the group is asked individually to rank what they see as the priority for one application against each of the others. So, against the expenses form and the global meetings calendar, the staff directory is seen as being more important (1 in the bottom section and 0 in the top section), but against the room booking form it is considered less important.

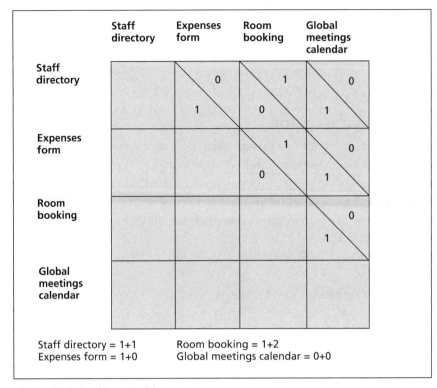

	Staff directory	Expenses form	Room booking	Global meetings calendar
Staff directory		0 / 1	1 / 0	0 / 1
Expenses form			1 / 0	0 / 1
Room booking				0 / 1
Global meetings calendar				

Staff directory = 1+1   Room booking = 1+2
Expenses form = 1+0   Global meetings calendar = 0+0

Figure 16.2 Ranking priorities

Overall, the scores given by this person show that they see Room Booking as the most important application to be developed. Summing the scores for the whole group should provide a ranked order of development that will then lead to a more interesting discussion and better informed agreement on priorities.

This approach can be very useful when looking at functionality trade-offs for CMS, search and social media applications. It is important not to take the scores as a definitive statement of the direction to be taken. All of these techniques provide a way of helping a group to reach a consensus on the development options.

A core governance model

There is no 'best' model for intranet governance, but I find that the model in Figure 16.3 is a good way to start the conversation.

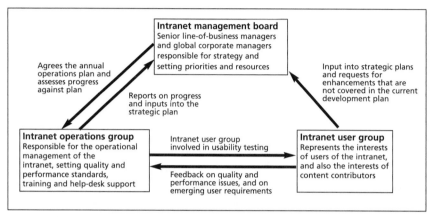

Figure 16.3 Intranet governance model

Intranet management board

The intranet management board is responsible for taking decisions that ensure that the intranet meets business needs and is integrated into the strategic planning cycle. It should have no more than about seven members. In line with the RACI approach set out above, there could well be others who act as advisors or consultants to the board, but there is no need to have a board of 12–15 people just so that it is 'representative'. The chairperson of the intranet user group and the intranet manager should both be ex-officio members of the board. I personally dislike the term 'steering group', which seems to imply setting a direction and objectives without having to take responsibility for allocating the resources to achieve the objectives.

Intranet operations group

The intranet operations group is chaired by the intranet manager and is responsible for implementing the operational plan. The intranet manager will also be an ex-officio member of the group, and can be present at meetings but will not have a vote. Other members of this group will include the IT help desk manager and some content contributors. The group should be able to call on advice from the HR and legal departments if required, but there is no requirement for them to be represented on the group.

Intranet user group

The intranet user group is a larger, and probably virtual, group that keeps track of usability issues, reports back to the intranet operations group on possible enhancements and helps to prioritize development plans. The input of this group to the planning effort is essential – it is a very determined senior manager who can sign off a business plan that is counter to the wishes of the intranet user group. Again, the intranet manager is an ex-officio member of the group, and should not object to being asked not to be present at a meeting or part of a meeting; users need to be able to comment and reach decisions without having to contend with the intranet manager becoming defensive about an issue. If the group feels strongly enough about the need for change then it should have the right to go direct to the intranet management board.

As part of good governance, each of these groups should have rules of procedure and a very clear indication of the types of decisions they are empowered to take. No one should be on the intranet management board unless they have a direct role in decision making. Keeping others informed or consulting them can be done in other ways than holding large meetings just for the purpose of information exchange.

Towards an annual governance cycle

In the early stages of intranet development the governance structure will probably be fairly easy to determine and will run quite well for a year or so. Then, as members of the intranet management board leave the organization or take on different roles, its focus and effectiveness will becomes increasingly diluted because newcomers will take up roles on the management board that they do not feel comfortable with or for which they have no clear charter from their department. Perhaps the line-of-business representative from networks will be replaced by a line-of-business representative from multimedia but the latter will have little previous experience of intranets, and in any case the requirements of the multimedia business are very different from those of other business units.

Rather than have an intranet management board with a permanent membership, there is much to be said for the membership changing in line with the annual review of the intranet strategy, the priorities that emerge and the detailed operational plans for the year. Continuity can be maintained by the intranet manager – probably the representative of the IT department – and, of course, by the intranet strategy itself.

Career development for the intranet team

No matter what overall governance structure is agreed, it is essential to ensure that the intranet manager has an appropriate line manager to report to who is in a position to carry out annual and other appraisals, sign off on leave and other requests and take responsibility for career development. Career development can be a challenging issue because there may be a temptation by a department to hold on to an intranet manager because of the potential difficulty of finding a replacement. The intranet manager then feels trapped and may well end up leaving the organization.

Resource

1   The approaches that organizations take to intranet governance are presented and analysed in the annual report from NetJMC *Global Intranet Trends*: http://netjmc.com/intranet-trends-report.

17

Developing an intranet strategy

Introduction

In Chapter 3 some of the considerations that need to be taken into account in writing a business plan for an intranet were set out, but the focus was on a tactical plan to be supported from the organization over perhaps the next financial year. Chapter 7, on selecting intranet CMS and search software, highlighted the potential need for a two-year perspective on funding the deployment of new software. This chapter takes an even longer-term view and looks at the benefits and challenges of preparing a two- or three-year strategy for an intranet.

Even quite large intranets may not be operating within a strategic plan, and yet employees rely every working day on information accessed from the intranet. Even if an individual employee has not accessed the intranet, their work for the day may well have been defined by a manager or a colleague who has done so. In most organizations, in terms of both the quantity and essential nature of the information, the intranet will have grown invisibly over its life, which may well stretch over many years.

Now, the intranet and the organization have reached a tipping point.
The current economic situation means that:

- staff are being made redundant and walking out of the door with
  invaluable knowledge about the organization
- staff who remain may well have to expand the scope of their work
  to accommodate the redundancies, and so have to access and trust
  information that they are not familiar with
- past business performance is no longer an indicator of the future,
  and new approaches will be needed so as to maintain and enhance
  customer relationships
- where new members of staff are hired, they will need to come up
  to speed and make a significant contribution to the organization as
  quickly as possible
- investment in IT applications will be under intense scrutiny.

All these factors play on the strengths of an intranet, which, compared
with most IT applications, requires little investment in hardware, software
or development. Intranet managers will be faced with some challenging
decisions in determining how best to prioritize development plans.

One of the complications that besets intranet investment decisions is
that the intranet is owned by a department – usually internal
communications, IT or HR – on behalf of the organization, but that
department has to maintain the intranet within its own departmental
budget. As a result, the role and scope of the intranet are often
constrained by the need to justify the intranet budget against the
objectives of the department, not of the organization as a whole.

Of course, there are notable exceptions to these generic and possibly
stereotyped views on intranet ownership, but the basic point is that the
intranet is not viewed as a strategic business application. There will be
strategic plans for the organization, individual departments or
subsidiaries, and for the investment cases for IT applications, but often
there is nothing similar for the intranet. The inevitable result is that the
intranet gradually and imperceptibly moves away from providing
effective support for the organization.

Unless a strategic plan is in place there is a very real danger that meeting ad hoc or short-term requirements will result in longer-term objectives being forgotten or not being clearly recognized. Another benefit of an intranet strategy is that it will hopefully ensure that decisions taken regarding other applications (perhaps upgrading an HR portal) recognize the impact that this could have on the intranet. Without a documented, visible strategy the dependences between the intranet and the HR portal may not be appreciated, even by the individual departments concerned.

Finally, with a strategy in place, and clear objectives and milestones for development decided, the intranet manager and the intranet team will have some equally clear career objectives. Without these it may be difficult to climb the internal promotion ladder, discuss conflicting job demands with a manager, or at a minimum gain some satisfaction for a job well done.

A structure for a strategy

When writing a strategy for an intranet it is very easy to work on a strategy for the current year and then roll it forward for the next two years. But very soon it will become obvious that there are too many unknowns to use the granularity that is essential for planning the current year as a structure for subsequent years.

This is where scenario planning can be very useful. A number of possible scenarios are presented, with an assessment of their probability of achievement and the factors that might have an impact on each scenario. For example, one scenario might assume that the organization will upgrade its HR system in two years and provide employee self-service applications. A second scenario might push this out to year three, relying on the intranet to develop some self-service applications that can then be migrated to the HR system in due course.

Attempting to develop these scenarios from a staff survey that includes questions such as 'Will you be making more use of social media in 2015?' is highly unlikely to produce any information and opinions of value. One approach that is worth considering is the Delphi methodology, in which individual 'experts' within the organization develop their own views of future scenarios in response to a questionnaire and these views are then further refined in one or more subsequent rounds. There is a very considerable body of literature on the subject.

In suggesting a structure for the strategy this book comes full circle and returns to the diagram used in Chapter 1 to highlight the value of an intranet to an organization (Figure 17.1). A strategic plan should set out how this value is going to be maintained over the period of the plan, with clear links into the organization's strategic plan.

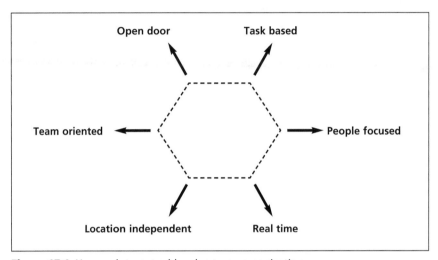

Figure 17.1 How an intranet adds value to an organization

To recap the elements of this model:

Open door – The intranet is a window into a wide a range of content and applications.

Task based – The intranet supports the completion of key tasks that have a direct impact on business performance.

People focused – The intranet should have excellent usability and support people making connections both inside and outside the organization.

Real time – The intranet should be as current as possible, so that users can trust the quality of the information they find.

Location independent – The intranet can be accessed on the premises of suppliers and customers, and over smart phones.

Team oriented – The intranet should support people working together, as that is the way in which decisions are now made in organizations that are risk aware.

These can then be translated into issues that need to be researched and presented in the strategy report (Table 17.1).

Table 17.1 Issues and strategies report	
Issue	**Strategy**
Front door	Will new or enhanced applications be implemented over the next 2–3 years that would ideally be integrated into the intranet?
	Would more customization or personalization be beneficial in meeting business and user requirements?
	Will there be requirements to provide increased access to the intranet for customers, contractors and suppliers?
Task based	How will the nature of work change in the organization?
	Will there be more self-service applications?
	Will some tasks be carried out across country boundaries?
	Could search functionality be embedded into tasks rather than being presented as a search box?
People focused	How will staff demographics change over the next three years, in terms of age, skills, location, role and responsibilities?
	How important will it be to support knowledge management initiatives?
	Where in the organization will there be a significant number of new employees?
	How could the intranet better support training and mentoring?
Real time	What is likely to be the value of social content and how will its quality be managed?
	Will there be an increased demand for rich-media support?
Location independent	What types of mobile devices will need to be supported?
	Will there be an increased requirement to support multiple languages?
Team oriented	What types of team will need to be supported in the future?
	Will these teams include participants from outside the organization?

Of course, these will not be the only questions, but they are intended to give an indication of the type of research that will need to be carried out across the organization. Many of these questions relate to what working practices will be like in the organization in the future, something that many organizations fail to consider.

Changing the way we work

Both the greatest opportunity and the greatest challenge for intranet managers will be to adapt the intranet to the way in which people will work in the future. Many research groups and consulting companies are now working on a range of projects on the future of work, and here the intranet team can take a lead in setting the agenda for an internal assessment of how their own organization will change working practices in the future.

One of the most challenging reports on enterprise information management in 2015 is by Accenture's *Information 2015: Reforming the paradigm*:[1]

> Today's unstructured content on most intranet portals is gathered and grouped manually. A central team decides on the information architecture and the content to include. When every piece of information within a company is annotated with metadata, applications or agents can autonomously gather and structure the content on a central information site. In this corporate semantic Web employees can start sophisticated search queries that are not possible with today's diffused and siloed information systems.
>
> Future employees will be able to create queries such as: 'Find me all of our research projects between 2010 and 2015 and give me the name of the respective project managers.' A vast amount of data in today's corporate intranets cannot be productively used: information remains undiscovered due to poor annotation and connections between information that is hidden deep within databases or on file servers. In the future, self-organizing approaches to derive value from unstructured content will gain greater significance.

The report goes on to propose four enterprise information scenarios for 2015:

Real-time reality mining – High-performance businesses analyse activity data about states and events in the physical and social world generated by sensors and the Internet of Things.

Augmented social workspaces – Social software will integrate with other platforms, mobile devices and spread towards the physical world.

Experts as a service – Winning organizations in 2015 will build up a network of experts offering a range of customer and business intelligence, reliably and in real time.

Personal decision engines – The personal decision engine will dramatically improve a company's ability to create concepts and develop solutions quickly and transparently.

These are all radical and challenging scenarios, and yet the report shows that they are in fact evolutionary scenarios based on current trends and fairly conservative technology forecasts. This is just one example of many such reports, and they should be essential reading for any intranet manager.

The proactive intranet

Historically, intranets have been implemented on a rather ad hoc basis to support existing business processes, with probably a primary alignment to the communications department. Over the last few years intranet development has had a stronger focus on identifying and supporting users' requirements for information and highly usable web applications. Now there is a significant opportunity for intranets to be proactive in supporting new working practices by working in tandem with the HR department and training professionals.

Resource

1   Accenture (2010) *Information in 2015: reforming the paradigm*, www.accenture.com/Global/Technology/Information_Mgmt/ Information_Mgmt_Services/R_and_I/Information-2015-Reforming.htm.

18
From intranets to information management

Introduction

In the final analysis, the reason why intranets fail is because organizations fail to understand the value of information as a business asset. Imagine for a moment that your company has built a factory and fitted it out with all the machinery needed to manufacture a new product. For any company that is a considerable investment. Or perhaps your company has built a large new office block with a sizeable car park and a good staff restaurant. Again, a considerable investment. Now I want you to imagine that it has forgotten where it built the factory and where the office is located. You will say that it is just impossible to imagine that. No company would be so incompetent.

Now imagine that over the last ten years you and your colleagues have been writing reports on competitors, market prospects, new products ideas and business strategies. All this information is stored somewhere on shared drives or in attached files on a Microsoft

Exchange server, but the people who stored the information have now left the company. Will you say that it is impossible to imagine that, and that your company would not be so incompetent? Unfortunately, this situation is much more common than you might imagine or even fear. Even where an intranet exists, corporate information is stored in multiple repositories – among which the intranet is just one.

There is now some hope that situations such as this will gradually become relics of the past. For much of the late 1990s, and on into the 21st century, there was considerable interest in (if little commitment to) the concepts and practice of knowledge management. Many considered that the post of chief knowledge officer was critical to the success of the organization. Few such officers now remain, though good practice in knowledge management is now well developed.

The fundamental problem that organizations failed to recognize was that without effective information management gaining a competitive advantage through knowledge management was very unlikely. Now the focus is turning to information management for competitive sustainability.[1,2]

Information management and information governance

The term 'information management' is becoming more widely used in management circles, but it seems to have no accepted definition. Indeed, while I was writing this book a search on Google for definitions of 'information management' yielded over two million hits. It seems to be one of those terms the meaning of which everyone knows – until they have to write down a definition and defend it. With the increasing interest in governance and compliance issues there is also a trend towards defining 'information management' in terms of 'information governance'.

The concept of information governance was given significant visibility in a 2008 report published by the Economist Intelligence Unit (EIU), entitled *The Future of Information Governance*.[3] In April 2008 the EIU conducted a survey among 192 senior executives around the world on the benefits, challenges and risks associated with developing an enterprise-wide information governance strategy. To supplement the findings of the survey, which was sponsored by EMC, the EIU also conducted in-depth interviews with a number of business executives from leading companies.

In their introduction to the report the authors wrote:

> While technology has been the focus of information management initiatives for some time, companies are beginning to realize that the full value of information depends in large part on the policies and procedures that govern and control its use, access, analysis, retention and protection. A corporation's capacity to handle information depends upon a variety of factors, including engaged executives and a company culture that supports collective ownership of information. However, strategically created enterprise-wide frameworks that define how information is controlled, accessed and used are arguably the most critical elements in a successful information management programme. For the purposes of this report, those frameworks – and the mechanisms that enforce them – are referred to as information governance.

The results of the survey make for interesting reading. Worldwide, nearly 73% of respondents reported that their company's overall ability to provide access to critical business information when needed was good or very good, and 65% said that their firm's ability to protect sensitive information was good or very good. However, only 38% of all respondents said that their companies have a formal enterprise-wide information governance strategy in place. In fact, less than half of all respondents believed that information governance was important or very important to their company's success. In the opinion of the EIU this suggested complacency among some companies about the true strategic importance of managing corporate information.

There are several reasons why proper information governance remains elusive, but the biggest challenge worldwide is identifying the cost/risk/return trade-offs of managing information company-wide (40%); enforcing policies company-wide (39%) and gaining support from department heads and line-of-business managers (35%) are also obstacles.

More positively, 77% of respondents expected information governance to be important or very important to their company's success over the next three years. As a result, many firms had begun building the foundation for information governance policies. A majority (65%) had defined policies regarding how information was to be stored and shared among employees and stakeholders. Furthermore, some organizations were appointing formal governance bodies to create strategies, policies and procedures for the distribution of information inside and outside the firm. This is a good start, but considering that 68% of respondents also expected that the complexity of their company's information governance issues would grow over the next three years, there is little time to waste.

Other findings from the survey include:

- Only 46% of respondents reported that their company's organizational structure for information governance was somewhat or very effective. Furthermore, only 54% of respondents said that their firm regularly reviewed and revised information back-up and retention policies. Moreover, when asked about managing the cost of collecting, storing and securing information throughout its life cycle, only 47% of respondents rated their firm's ability in this area as good or very good.
- As a result, sharing data across a company remains difficult. Only 43% of respondents rated their firm's ability to integrate and share information across departments and necessary third parties as good or very good; 21% said that it was poor or very poor. This is particularly significant, as it pertains to sharing customer information: 57% of respondents acknowledged that they did not have a clear idea of the customer.
- Those who had a formal information governance strategy reported significant benefits. More than four-fifths (81%) of firms with a formal information governance strategy in place reported that 'information can be better shared between departments, allowing for better decision-making'. Nearly half (47%) of respondents from these firms also said that 'integrated information and business intelligence about our customers, products and resources can be leveraged for greater business results'.

- For firms without a governance strategy, the risks may be significant. Only 51% of respondents at companies that did not have a formal information governance strategy rated their firm's overall ability to protect sensitive data as good or very good, compared with 85% for those whose companies had a formal strategy.
- Similarly, 92% of respondents at firms with information governance strategies rated their company's ability to provide access to critical business information when needed as good or very good, compared with only 57% of companies that did not have governance strategies in place.

Figure 18.1 illustrates the problem that we are facing. The top solid line is an indication of how rapidly information repositories are expanding, and yet the spend on IT is at best only going to match inflation [bottom line]. The capacity of staff to manage the information they need is not keeping up with the growth [double line]. Three actions need to be taken:

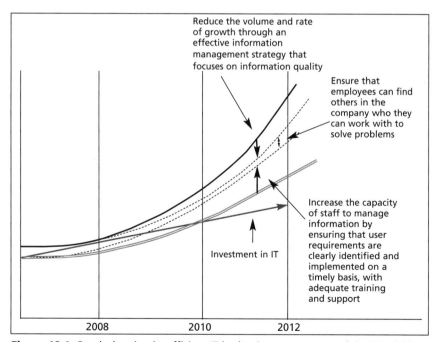

Figure 18.1 Graph showing insufficient IT budgeting to meet growth in IT activities

1   An information management strategy will start to address issues of information volume by focusing on information quality and relevance.
2   At the same time user requirements for information will be better defined, so that solutions can be put into place which will facilitate the management of information.
3   The gap that will still remain will be filled by ensuring that people can make connections with others both inside and outside the organization.

These actions need to be addressed within an information management strategy.

The implications for an intranet strategy

In the intranet world, as in so many other areas of activity, less can be more. It is important to be able to distinguish between 'fitness to specification' and 'fitness to purpose'. Intranets can quickly become dumping grounds for information that does not seem to fit in other applications, and this is where an overall information management strategy can of great value because it can establish norms for quality that apply across the organization, and therefore to the intranet.

A business has three main assets: its employees, its reputation and its information. Great care will be taken of the employees, everyone will be mindful of maintaining its reputation, but no one will have overall responsibility for the information assets of the business. If there is no coherent understanding and support for information management in an organization, then any attempt to produce an intranet strategy is going to be a significant challenge, and implementing the strategy will be very difficult. The larger the organization, the greater the challenge, as the more complex will be the array of related applications that in some way may need to interface with the intranet.

Some organizations have set up enterprise information architecture approaches. These start with high-level business definitions and descriptions, setting standards for data throughout the organization. Certainly standard, common metadata definitions are key to establishing proper communication, including the concept of standard formats for messages between processes, but the scope of this work tends to focus on data and databases, and not on information in a wider sense.

Often the reason why an organization has not developed an information management strategy is that no one knows quite where to begin. Set out in the final section of this chapter is a framework an information management strategy that could be a starting point for a discussion about the scope, objectives and principles of such a strategy.

An information charter

I take a user-centric model of information management. If an organization has an effective information management strategy, then all of its employees should be able to say:

- I can find the information I need.
- I trust the information I find.
- I can publish information for others to use.
- I am able to share my expertise.
- My manager supports my information responsibilities.
- My networks extend beyond the firewall.

This is quite a challenging charter. Typically, I use it in presentations to senior management groups. Each item is displayed in sequence and I ask the attendees to raise their hands if they are in agreement with the principle. There is usually unanimous agreement on the first four items, some abstentions on the fifth and agreement on the sixth 'so long as that does not imply we need to give our employees access to Facebook'.

I then present all six points, and ask if attendees would be willing to post the charter on the intranet as an aspiration for the next 12 months. This is at present a step too far, but there is now certainly more interest in having a discussion around 'information management' than there was a couple of years ago.

For organizations that subscribe to the services of Gartner, this is because Gartner has been at the forefront of promoting information governance and provides a toolkit for clients to use when assessing their information management capabilities and practices.

In a note to clients in late 2009, Gartner advised:

> To obtain maximum value from your information assets you must make organizational changes. Information stewards, governance teams and information managers are roles that must be filled and shared between IT and business units. If you have an enterprise architecture function begin to expand its scope and skill base to structure information assets at a more detailed level. Begin working with business units to get them to understand that they will need to staff positions that deal directly with information; its creation, use and life cycle. Hire information managers, records managers, digital archivists, and legal IT professionals, and cross train them.

A framework for an information management strategy

This section sets out an information management strategy I developed for a multinational company. It should not be taken as a definitive approach, but only as an illustration of the scope of an IM strategy:

1 Information quality
2 Workflow processes and procedures
3 Discovery
4 Personalization and customization
5 Staff recruitment and retention
6 Location-independent access
7 Global capability
8 Language diversity
9 Support for collaborative working
10 Training and education.

Information quality
Requirement

Often we have multiple versions of documents in different repositories. Staff may not have the knowledge to be able to find all the available versions and then decide which is the definitive version. We have to ensure that it is easy to locate and identify the definitive version of any document, and who is the author of the document.

Information is a corporate asset. It is not something that 'belongs' to an individual or a directorate, but is managed by them on behalf of the organization. Therefore all information should have an owner who will be the guardian of the information on behalf of ABC and will be responsible for ensuring that:

- the information is complete, accurate and up to date
- there is a procedure for correcting inaccurate information
- the information is made available to anyone within ABC who has a legitimate 'need to know'
- any security requirements associated with the information are complied with
- any long-term retention requirements associated with the information are identified
- access under compliance and regulatory requirements is facilitated.

Actions

1.1 We will develop procedures to progressively review and, where appropriate, discard low-value information so that over time the quality of the information held by ABC is progressively enhanced.

1.2 We will develop guidelines that will assist employees in raising the quality and relevance of the information they create and share.

1.3 We will provide staff with a single point of access to internal and external information resources, recognizing when individual employees or groups of employees need to be alerted to specific information as it becomes available.

1.4 We will undertake regular surveys of employees so that we can maintain and, where possible, enhance the excellence of our information and knowledge resources, systems and training.

1.5 We will ensure that the copyright and other intellectual property rights of both ABC and other companies are recognized and complied with.

1.6 We will develop a framework for the implementation and governance of social software applications, and establish guidelines for the use of internal blogs and wikis.

Workflow processes and procedures
Requirement

We have well-defined workflows and procedures for the majority of business-critical processes. We need to understand the role of information in the successful completion of a workflow or procedure. This will reduce information overload, enhance productivity and empower staff to make the best possible business decisions, and in doing this we will also reduce business risk.

Actions

2.1 We will ensure that, based on user research, staff are provided with only that information which is needed to successfully complete a specific stage of the workflow.

2.2 We will differentiate between information to which they should be alerted and information that they will search for as required.

Discovery
Requirement

Over at least the last decade ABC has created probably millions of terabytes of information. Even older information may impact on current or future business. Staff need to be able to locate this information in a variety of ways, including navigation schemes in web applications, file plans in document management applications and folder structures on shared drives. Enterprise search has an important role to play but is not necessarily the solution to all information discovery requirements, many of which need to be supported by the ability to browse through related collections of information using classification schemes, taxonomies and links. It is also important that service selection, based either on the preferences of the user or developed to meet the needs of groups of users, is provided.

Actions

3.1 We will ensure that the information discovery applications are applicable to the ways in which staff will approach the identification of information.

3.2 We will develop appropriate navigation, classification and taxonomy schemes to support the process of information discovery.

3.3 We will recognize the difference between the requirement for *some* relevant information and the requirement to be able to locate *all* relevant information in support of specific tasks.

Personalization and customization
Requirement

It is very easy for staff to be overwhelmed by the volume of information that is available to them. Solutions to this are to provide staff with:

Customized information services that support the requirements of groups of staff performing specific roles, or working on specific tasks

Personalized information services which enable an individual to select information that they wish to be alerted to as it becomes available.

These services need to accommodate a wide range of circumstances, including:

- the employee's knowledge of the available range of information resources from which to make a selection
- the language skills and educational background of the employee
- the employee's experience to know the value of the information that they find
- the rate at which information is added or revised
- whether the information is internally or externally sourced.

Actions

4.1 We will develop methodologies that can be used in the design, implementation and maintenance of customized and personalized information resources.

4.2 We will develop training courses to ensure that staff are confident in their ability to use these systems.

4.3 We will ensure that staff are informed about the availability of new or enhanced services and are offered alternatives to discontinued services.

Staff recruitment and retention
Requirement

Employees now regard the desktop and the network as their working space. Increasingly, employees will view applications developed for the consumer market as essential in their business life. We must offer these employees an information environment which will be the envy of any company that they might consider working for. New members of staff must be able to contribute their expertise at the earliest possible opportunity in their employment.

When employees leave ABC we will ensure that they are able to identify and review the major contributions they have made to ABC so there is a definitive legacy of their work and experience on which others can build.

We will support staff recruitment and retention by ensuring that our strategies for information, expertise and knowledge management are at least as good as, and ideally better than, our major competitors', recognizing that not all staff will be recruited from the pharmaceutical sector.

Actions

5.1 We will support the development of training courses in personal information management.

Location-independent access
Requirement
Our staff work around the world both in ABC offices and in meetings with suppliers and providers. We must ensure that there are no technical or organizational barriers to accessing information from any global location, so that decisions can be made on a timely basis.

Actions
6.1 We will conduct a survey that identifies the barriers to location-independent access and assess the business value of finding solutions to these barriers.

6.2 We will ensure that the intranet provides as much information as possible to assist employees who need to access internal ABC resources whilst working away from their own office.

Global capability
Requirement
A major competitive advantage of ABC is the knowledge of its staff. This needs to be made available to all who need it. We also need to ensure that the knowledge gained by staff is not lost when they leave the company.

Actions
7.1 We will support the continued development of harmonized staff directories and their progressive enhancement into a global expertise directory.

7.2 We will support the development of a procedure to ensure that when employees leave the company important information assets that they have created are allocated to others for ownership.

Language diversity
Requirement
We will continue to work in many different languages but this should

not be a barrier to staff accessing information in a language that they do not understand either fully or partially.

Actions

8.1 We will ensure that employees, especially those new to ABC or taking up a new position, have access to information in any language and location so that they can make an immediate and long-lasting contribution to ABC and accelerate their career development.

Support for collaborative working
Requirement

Employees should be able to identify and share knowledge and expertise so that they can respond as quickly as possible to business opportunities and challenges.

Because, in this increasingly unpredictable and competitive environment, good decisions are invariably made collectively we will provide a range of secure IT applications that are intuitive to use from any location, including those of customers and suppliers.

We need to support the provision of information to teams, groups and committees to ensure that the decisions of those bodies are made known to all who have a need and the authority to use this information.

Actions

9.1 Define the requirements for communication, co-operation, collaboration and connection between teams.
9.2 Ensure that staff are trained in the use of IT applications that support these activities.

Training and education
Requirement

It will be essential to train staff at all levels in the principles of information management, particularly in publishing and, by this means, sharing information, taking responsibility for updating information and ensuring that it is archived according to corporate procedures.

Actions

10.1 Promote ownership of information throughout the organization, whilst making information accessible where appropriate.

10.2 Develop an ABC-wide approach to raising awareness of the importance and implications of information management.

10.3 Define key competencies in information management for specific roles and incorporate these skills into job descriptions and evaluations, and also into personal review plans.

Resources

1 There are a number of books that address the challenges organizations face in managing information as an asset, including:
Boiko, B. (2007) *Laughing at the CIO*, Medford, NJ: Information Today Inc.
Evernden, R. and Evernden, E. (2003) *Information First*, London: Butterworth-Heinemann.
Marchand, D. A. (2000) *Competing with Information*, New York: Wiley.
Orna, E. (1999) *Practical Information Policies*, London: Gower Publishing.
Orna, E. (2004) *Information Strategy in Practice*, London: Gower Publishing.

2 Socitm, a UK organization representing IT professionals in the public sector, published a report in 2010 setting out an information life-cycle approach to the development of an information management strategy: *Managing Information: managing the lifeblood of the organisation*, www.socitm.net/insight.

3 Economist Intelligence Unit (2008) *The Future of Information Governance*, www.eiuresources.com/mediadir/default.asp?PR=2008102001.

Appendix A – Guidelines for social media use

There are many published guidelines on the internal use of social media, of which those from IBM and Intel are widely recognized as setting a high standard. This set of guidelines, in alphabetical order, has been developed from a number of different sources.

Adding value

It should always be clear what value your contribution is adding to the business. Be informative and interesting. Your expertise, experience and opinions regarding issues you know well and care about could have a significant impact on the performance of the business.

Anger management

It is very easy for people to use social media to sound off about something. If there is a critical edge to a contribution, come back and look at it again and imagine how you would react if you were the recipient of the posting. Once the words are out there, you cannot get them back, and once an inflammatory discussion gets going the damage can be widespread and long lasting.

Anonymity

All contributions should be signed, and that includes comments.

Readers may wish to find out more about you, so make sure your entry in the staff directory is current and relevant.

Approval

There is no approval process for social media within the organization, but it is courteous to inform your manager, and also your colleagues, that you are contributing to a social media channel. You would not want them to be unaware that you were doing so, and be surprised to find that others in the organization were reading your report of a department meeting.

Circulation

You may be making contributions to a blog or wiki to which access is currently restricted to either specific employees or employees with a specific role or function. It is sometimes easy to forget that this is the case and that your contribution may be invisible to many people who could benefit from it. It is also worth remembering that it is still possible for your contribution to escape if someone wishes to circulate it to others. And, some time in the future the social media application, and your contributions to it, could be opened up to a much wider audience than you originally envisaged.

Comments

There should always be a right of reply within the same media channel so that there is an audit trail. A comment by e-mail may not be seen by all the readers of an internal blog. Always pause and think before posting a reply, and respond to comments in a timely manner, even if just to acknowledge the effort that others have made in providing comments. Their time is as valuable as yours.

Compliance

Make sure that you are aware of all compliance issues, especially if there are any e-discovery implications. Compliance requirements may be different in some countries, and it is up to you to make the effort to check on what is permissible. The legal department is the definitive source of information on compliance requirements.

Confidentiality

It is often difficult within an organization to recognize what information is confidential. If in doubt, do not publish, or seek authority to do so. Some customers and suppliers may have access to some social media applications, and even if they do not someone may inadvertently reveal information that you have posted about them. Never disclose any operational performance information about the organization.

Context

People have multiple roles in organizations. They might be a member of a department, a representative on a worker's council and a project manager. When using social media make sure that it is clear to readers in what context you are publishing your contribution.

Conversation

Talk to your readers in the same way that you would do in a meeting. Especially in international organizations, readers may have difficulty reading complex sentence constructions or understanding slang or jargon. If you are seen to encourage comment, then your message will travel farther and have more weight from the peer review. Make sure that you identify others who are blogging about the same topic, so that readers get a range of opinions.

Copyright

Be aware of the laws governing copyright if you are referring to content from an external website, a published report or a book.

Cultural sensitivity

People from many cultures around the world would be very uncomfortable in openly criticizing a manger or a corporate policy. Muslim and non-Muslim countries have different work-weeks, and every country has different public holidays. Off-hand comments about the availability of people or a delay in receiving responses might be regarded as objectionable or, at the very least, insensitive.

Disclaimer

Always be very open about who are you, and to what extent are your views your own, those of colleagues you work with or of the organization as a whole: 'This is the personal blog of [Name] and contains my personal views, thoughts and opinions. These opinions should not be considered to be those of my colleagues or the organization itself.'

It can be helpful to include an e-mail address or a telephone number so that a colleague can contact you directly if they have a query or concern about the posting. It is important that managers and senior executives consider whether the personal thoughts they publish might be misunderstood as being corporate opinion, and any manager should assume that their team will either read what is written or find out about it indirectly.

Discretion

Do not discuss topics of which you have no direct knowledge. If you're about to publish something that you feel may be misunderstood, then it probably will be. Take a break and review the posting, focusing on perhaps just a sentence that concerns you. If you're still unsure, discuss it with a colleague or a manager. Ultimately, what you publish has your name on it and your reputation across the organization is at stake. Do not make reference to customers, contractors or suppliers without their approval.

Engagement

Make sure you read the contributions of others. Only through being aware of these conversations will you be able to assess whether you have a contribution to make.

Expertise

You may think you are an expert. Others may disagree. Don't be overbearing in the way you communicate your expertise. You could be wrong. If you are writing about a topic that the organization is involved with but you are not yourself an expert on that topic, you should make this clear to your readers.

Honesty

If you get something wrong be prepared to apologize. Tell the truth, and if you find you have made a mistake, issue a clarification or a withdrawal, whatever may suit the circumstance, and make it abundantly clear that you have done so. In a blog, if you choose to modify an earlier post, make it clear that you are doing so. The nature of social communication is that mistakes and errors occur, but in social media you will not see the body language that might alert you to a problem or a lack of understanding. If you have a vested interest in something you are discussing, declare this in the opening sentences, not at the end of a contribution.

Language

In a multinational organization the corporate language should be used if possible. For various reasons it may be more appropriate to use the local language, but in that case provide a title in the corporate language and a brief summary of the contribution.

Links

People should be able to link back to a specific contribution, and not have to go to the complete blog or wiki.

Opinions

You have yours. Others will have theirs. Always respect them. What you publish will be around for a long time and your opinion may change.
Personal privacy

In the EU, and in a number of other countries, there is legislation on data privacy. It is in the nature of social media that personal comments become interleaved with business comments. However, a passing reference to welcoming a colleague back from a stay in hospital might prejudice a future employment opportunity for them. Make sure that you are conversant with data protection legislation, but the best approach is never to include personal information about a colleague.

Personal responsibility

Disclaimers will not let you get away with ill-considered contributions.

Quality

Make your contribution concise. A good benchmark is that readers should not have more than a one-and-a-half-page scroll. Be sure to check your facts and figures – if you don't, someone else probably will and whatever opinion you have expressed will then be open to question.

Readership

Some internal social media applications may permit suppliers and business partners to participate, so be sensitive to who will see your content.

Sarcasm

Sarcasm is never an acceptable approach to conversations, and this is especially the case in written communications, where the tone of voice is irrelevant.

Timeliness

If you need a comment by a particular time, be clear about this in the blog or wiki.

Titles

Many people like to create very 'clever' titles for their blogs, but in corporate social media the aim is to communicate, not to impress. The same is true for the heading of each contribution. Search engines almost always place relevance emphasis on a title, and people browsing through a number of blogs and discussion groups need a good title, so as to know when to read the rest of the post.

Versions

Rather than editing your content once it has been published, find ways to make your corrections transparent.

Work/life balance

Networking and communicating using social media can be time consuming and it is important that it does not interfere with work for your organization. If the business would benefit from your posting on a more regular or more lengthy basis than the working day allows, this is something that you should discuss with your manager.

Index

More Titles of Interest
from Information Today, Inc.

Information Nation
Education and Careers in the Emerging Information Professions

By Jeffrey M. Stanton, Indira R. Guzman, and Kathryn R. Stam

Information and IT are central to virtually every industry in which the United States plays a leadership role yet colleges have failed to attract, teach, and produce a new generation of information professionals to meet the growing need. Here, three dedicated educators present research on students and workers in the information professions, highlighting barriers to inclusion and retention, analyzing the forces that prevent high school and college students from getting the interdisciplinary skills they need, and telling the stories of a diverse group of students who are thriving in new majors and new jobs.

256 pp/softbound/ISBN 978-1-57387-401-4/$35.00

Intranets for Info Pros

Edited by Mary Lee Kennedy and Jane Dysart

The intranet is among the primary landscapes in which information-based work occurs, yet many info pros view it with equal parts skepticism and dread. In *Intranets for Info Pros*, editors Kennedy and Dysart and 10 expert contributors provide a wealth of advice and support for the information professional charged with implementing or contributing to an intranet.

Leading thinkers and practitioners contributing to *Intranets for Info Pros* are Angela Abell, Avi Rappoport, Jose Claudio Terra, Cory Costanzo, Craig St. Clair, Cynthia Ross Pedersen, Debra Wallace, Eric Hards, Ian Littlejohn, and Mike Crandall. Together with Kennedy and Dysart, they demonstrate the intranet's strategic value, describe important trends and best practices, and equip info pros to make a key contribution to their organization's intranet success.

304 pp/softbound/ISBN 978-1-57387-309-3/$39.50

Implementing Technology Solutions in Libraries
Techniques, Tools, and Tips From the Trenches

By Karen C. Knox

For anyone seeking a straightforward, hands-on approach to implementing technology solutions in libraries, this is your guide! Created for staff who want to ensure success with a technology project that may consume a significant part of the library's budget, author and IT manager Karen Knox deconstructs an entire project implementation, from planning to evaluation, carefully examining each step.

The author has implemented many technology projects over the years—some more successfully than others, as she is quick to admit. Here, she draws on her experience to help readers identify the most critical components of any project while modifying and scaling to meet their library's unique needs. The array of tips, tricks, techniques, and tools she shares here are designed to spell success in your next library technology implementation.

192 pp/softbound/ISBN 978-1-57387-403-8/$35.00

Knowledge Management in Practice
Connections and Context

Edited by T. Kanti Srikantaiah and Michael E. D. Koenig

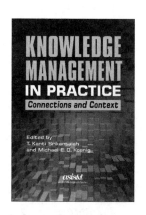

This third entry in the ambitious, highly regarded KM series from editors Srikantaiah and Koenig features 26 chapters contributed by more than 20 experts from around the globe. The book not only looks at how KM is being implemented in organizations today, but is unique in surveying the efforts of KM professionals to extend knowledge beyond their organizations and in providing a framework for understanding user context. *Knowledge Management in Practice* is a must-read for any professional seeking to connect organizational KM systems with increasingly diverse and geographically dispersed user communities.

544 pp/hardbound/ISBN 978-1-57387-312-3
ASIST Members $47.60 • Nonmembers $59.50

To order or for a complete catalog, contact:
Information Today, Inc.
143 Old Marlton Pike, Medford, NJ 08055 • 609/654-6266
email: custserv@infotoday.com • Web site: www.infotoday.com